Generalate
Sister Magdalena Krol OSF

SISTERS OF ST. FRANCIS
OF PERPETUAL ADORATION, OLPE

150 YEARS
for-with-by-one another

Éditions du Signe

CONTENTS

150 YEARS
for-with-by-one another

FOREWORD

Dear Sisters, dear readers!

Jubilees are times of remembrance and celebration of those who built what we continue today. That is why, in the first place, I would like to thank our older Sisters. With their loyalty to our Community, they have created a solid basis for us today.

I am thankful to everyone who, over the decades, has worked with us and helped to shape our institutions in the different Provinces, namely:

the *"Charitable Association of the Franciscans of Olpe"*, Germany; the *"Franciscan Alliance"*, *"University of St. Francis"*, Mishawaka, USA; the *"Franciscan Healthcare Corporation"*, Colorado Springs, USA; *"Franciscan College of the Immaculate Conception College"*, Baybay, the Philippines; and the *"Sonho de Aline"* project in São José de Ribamár, Brazil.

I am filled with happiness and hope when I think of all the young Sisters in the different Provinces who have joined us today and continue to walk in the footsteps of Christ and St. Francis.

We have recognized our Mother Maria Theresia Bonzel's spirit through the decades. She influenced not only the Sisters of her generation but also we who have followed her example much later.

In the 150 years since our Community's foundation, much has changed in the appearance of the Community. However, our identity remains the same. We have not become younger, and yet what is still important to us is *"to adore and to work,"* to create *"an option for God and the people"* and *"to adore and work in the spirit of mercy."* For 138 years in the United States, 51 years in the Philippines and 50 years in Brazil, every Sister has striven toward these goals according to her own strengths and abilities.

We share our concerns about resources with many Communities in Germany and the United States. We do not want to speculate about what tomorrow will bring because we will never know. Tomorrow remains in God's hands, and if there is a place for us in it, we will take it. Our foundress Mother Maria Theresia Bonzel summarized her life as follows:

"He (God) leads; I follow." As we are responsible for today, we stay on Mother Maria Theresia Bonzel's path and fashion it in our own way with the decisions we make every day of our lives.

The purpose of this commemorative booklet is to invite you to join us to pause and reflect, to share memories and impressions. We would also like to pass on Mother Maria Theresia Bonzel's encouraging words in one of her letters:

"Everything is in God's hands; and if we do what we can, we can be at peace."

Sr. Magdalena Krol OSF
General Superior

"HE LEADS, I FOLLOW"

USA

BRAZIL

PHILIPPINES

OLPE

6

USA   PHILIPPINES   BRAZIL

A GUIDE THROUGH THIS BOOKLET

All the authors who have contributed to this booklet feel a deep connection with Mother Maria Theresia Bonzel, the foundress of the Sisters of St. Francis of Perpetual Adoration. One hundred fifty years have passed since the Community's foundation — a good reason to recall Mother Maria Theresia's life and work. It is also an occasion to follow the traces she has left for future generations, as well as to pause, reflect, and celebrate this jubilee together. Celebrations are vital in our lives so that we do not get lost in everyday duties and affairs but learn to recognize what is essential for us with the help of role models such as Mother Maria Theresia. In this booklet the authors have tried to extract from Mother Maria Theresia's life and work what *"really matters"* to us today.

The team of authors is aware that not all aspects of Mother Maria Theresia's personality and work can be included in this booklet. Yet we have still tried to show you, dear readers, Mother Maria Theresia's legacy from different angles.

To Adore and to Work is the booklet's title. The thread that connects the different chapters is also Mother Maria Theresia's guiding principle: *"He (God) leads — I follow."* Adoration gave the Sisters the strength to help where need was greatest, and knowing that God leads, the Sisters could and still can face the challenges of every era. They are thankful for their successes, yet are able to place the impossible in God's hands during daily adoration and to trust that God's abilities are greater than their own.

The first chapter looks at Mother Maria Theresia's life and work in relation to our time, 150 years after the Community's foundation. Our aim is to find what "really matters" in our lives today.

The second chapter presents an overview of Mother Maria Theresia's work.

The life of the Community after Mother Maria Theresia's death is the focus of the third chapter.

The fourth chapter takes a look at the time of German re-unification in 1989, when the borders of the German Democratic Republic (GDR) were opened, and at the personal experiences of the Sisters in a Thuringian province, who witnessed events first-hand and close up.

Chapters 5 and 6 are dedicated to the Motherhouse in Olpe, which literally acted and continues to act as a "mother" to the Sisters, as the home they have left to spread the Gospel to all corners of the world. It is a place of true "woman power" where all the Sisters from the different Provinces have met and continue to meet regularly.

In Chapters 7 to 10 the different overseas Provinces belonging to the Community are introduced: how they were established, how they developed, what life is like today, and what kind of work is carried out in the different locations.

Chapter 11 is headlined "To Adore and to Pray" — it affords a glimpse into the Sisters' spirituality.

Chapter 12 is dedicated to the "Charitable Association of the Franciscans of Olpe," which was established in 1995 with the motto "Yes to Dignity!" in order to safeguard Mother Maria Theresia Bonzel's legacy in the face of an aging and declining membership. Interviews illustrate the traces Mother Maria Theresia has left, even on down to our present time, which are being followed by the Association's competent work.

To conclude, Chapters 13 and 14 consist of interviews with the oldest and the youngest Sister, respectively.

Under "On the Lighter Side" and "Aline Wants to Know," we catch some humorous glimpses into the Sisters' lives. See the explanations in "How to use this booklet".

We, the team of authors, hope that you will find insight, perspective, food for thought, joy, and courage in this booklet.

→ Another suggestion on how to use this booklet: for humor and relaxation, you will find "Aline Wants to Know" and "On the Lighter Side" scattered throughout the booklet.

Aline wants to know

Aline is a girl who has been studying at St. Francis High School in Olpe for one year. Together with other boys and girls from her class, she has collected questions for the Sisters.

However, these are not just children's questions. Adults may simply shy away from asking them. Perhaps some of you will find the answers you have always been looking for here.

We have named the girl Aline in recognition of Mother Maria Theresia's birth name. Her middle names were Regina Christine Wilhelmine. Not only did everyone lovingly call her Aline, but she also used the name herself later on.

That is why this name is being used when naming institutions. Our curious Aline was also wondering about that.

On the Lighter Side

Our Community's 150-year history has seen many a funny moment. We are certain that, had we conducted a survey, we would have been able to fill another book.

In *"On the Lighter Side"* we look at the memories and anecdotes of two of our Sisters. Sister Robertann Lathrop from Mishawaka, USA, has collected many wonderfully amusing stories from her long teaching career in her booklet *"Teaching Days vs. Teaching Daze."* They are complemented by the memories of Sister Josefa Teschner from Oschersleben, Germany, who has experienced many a surprise relating to the children's biblical creativity during her work as parish liaison officer.

The ability to see the funny side of life amidst all its seriousness is part of Franciscan spirituality. Records from the life of St Francis himself and stories from Mother Maria Theresia's life pay testimony to this. Every single one of us is very likely to have experienced it in our own lives, too.

In difficult situations it often helps to look on the bright side.

"He
leads
–

FOLLOW"

I

13

CONVENT IN THE MOTHERHOUSE

Dear Mother Maria Theresia,

"Heaven is everything!" was the motto of the 75 years of your life! Heavenward! You gave this longing for Heaven a shape when you founded the Sisters of St. Francis of Perpetual Adoration. One hundred fifty years have passed since the foundation — an important enough occasion for us to celebrate this jubilee. We are sure that you would reject any kind of praise. You felt passionately about *"forgetting the self:"* everything for the honor of God; nothing for the honor of man. No, you do not need a jubilee, but perhaps we do. What you started back then still has significant meaning in our time, even more so since belief in Heaven seems to have been lost. That is why we need people like you, people for whom *"Heaven is everything."*

Pope Benedict XVI's encyclical *"Caritas in Veritate"* says: *"Man without God does not know where to go, and neither does he know who he is."* While you, dear Mother Maria Theresia, centered your life on God, "man without God" is visibly gaining ground. According to official statistics, one third of all Germans claim to be without religion. All over the world, more than one billion people are non-believers. In your time, religion played a much more important role in people's lives — even though the skeptical voices of Nietzsche, Marx, Freud, the *"masters of criticism of religion"* could already be heard. Karl Marx coined the famous phrase: *"Religion is the opium of the people."* Friedrich Nietzsche asked: *"Where is God?"* and told the *"great people"* that *"God is dead."*

MOTHER MARIA THERESIA BONZEL

You can imagine the consequences: for the *"man without God"* generation, the mercilessness of life seems even harsher. They strive for everything that is worth striving for in the short time between birth and death. Those who cannot keep up lose out. The creation of a society without suffering, without illness and disability, without the impertinence of aging, acts as a replacement for God. The more man becomes his own experiment, the colder the world gets. One contemporary says: *"It is about doing without other-worldly promises, about risking looking life straight in the face."* Another sees belief as intellectual bankruptcy: *"I accept the fact that there is no higher purpose in life."* For a fairly significant part of humanity, God does not matter anymore in the 21st century. Rather, people rely on their own experiences or on scientific principles.

However, if God is dead, *"Where does Man go?"* Nietzsche asked. What will happen to the inde-structible desire for *"more,"* the desire to *"live"* beyond death? Many might agree with the writer Michel Houellebecq: *"My non-belief is a white room, murky, in which one can only move with the greatest effort, eternal winter."* An eternal winter not followed by spring, which encourages us to just keep on going, without any solace or anchor. What has happened to us? What have we done to ourselves?

Dear Mother Maria Theresia, we are trying to approach you from this background of religious detachment. We celebrate you as our foundress in a time that revolves only around itself. Could your life and work in the 19th century lead us the way through the 21st century?

"Olpe Has Seen a Star" —
Your Quiet Path:
Adoration and Mercy

Your contemporaries have passed away. Yet in their letters they repeatedly point out your unique charisma. They revered you as a woman deeply anchored in her belief and her love for God, who drew her strength from this intense relationship with Him and who faced the challenges of her time with great courage. Even without official recognition, your Community venerates you as a saint. To this day, all

Aline wants to know

Why do you wear a golden ring?

The golden ring is a symbol of my commitment to live as a Franciscan all my life. It is like a "bridal ring." The Community stands by me and I stand by the Community.

Sisters of St. Francis of Perpetual Adoration in all Provinces are committed to your principles.

Yours was a quiet path — you kept a low profile. You withdrew to prayer and meditation as often as possible — it was your source of strength. At the same time you possessed a sober sense of reality that allowed you to make wise decisions. Your knowledge of human nature, and your sharp eye, which often uncovered the most secret of thoughts, left a lasting impression on your contemporaries. *"Once experienced, she can never be forgotten"* (Sister Francesco Brüggemann).

"The way we pray is the way we live; our life is our prayer."

Even as a young girl you felt that *"God wants all my heart."* Right to the end you made yourself available to God and overcame all obstacles in your way without ever losing courage, because you knew that God was looking after you. Your trust in His lead and love was unshakeable. Like every human relationship, a relationship with God needs to be nurtured. For you, this meant a daily conversation with God. The deeper the connection a person establishes with Him through prayer, the richer his humanity becomes.

On the Lighter Side

My teaching career began in 1948 as a substitute in the 8th grade classroom for the last two weeks of May. That experience really rings "a bell" in my collection of memories. I stood before the class of teenagers, trying to look brave and "on top" of the situation. I soon found out there is a clown in every classroom. A boy of popular status among his classmates decided to put on a few "shows." The class enjoyed his humor, and mistakenly, I joined in the laughter! It lasted a little too long. To stop the nonsense, I said to the class: "We better get down to business; it's like a zoo in here"! Sure enough, Jim spoke up and exclaimed — "And just think, Sister, you didn't have to pay to get in!"

STATUE OF ST FRANCIS, MISHAWAKA

You measured your own actions against Jesus Christ's; He was at the center of your deeds. In this way, your life became prayer and your prayer — life. For you, praying meant letting the soul breathe. What your namesake Teresa of Avila said about prayer applied to you as well: *"Praying means talking to a friend whom we enjoy meeting often and alone for a conversation because we know that he loves us."*

CHAPEL OF PERPETUAL ADORATION IN THE PHILIPPINES

CHAPEL OF PERPETUAL ADORATION IN BRAZIL

You accepted adversity and suffering as a way of carrying the suffering of Christ and man. Through prayer you survived periods of drought, attacks and injustice. You overcame self-centeredness because the *"cross-beam of our own self-will completes the cross."* You wanted God to rule over you and use you as an instrument useful to Him. *"Having no desire greater than wishing and wanting what God asks of us,"* you placed great importance on contemplative life in your Community. You took turns to spend time in front of the tabernacle, hour by hour, day by day, night by night, to reconnect with Him to whom you gave your life.

For you, prayer acted as a balance to, as well as a preparation for, confrontation with the many economic and social changes taking place at the time as a result of industrialization, which led to mass poverty

CHAPEL OF PERPETUAL ADORATION IN COLORADO SPRINGS

CHAPEL OF PERPETUAL ADORATION IN OLPE

for whole strata of the population. Unbelievable suffering and early deaths ensued. You were shocked by all this. When Bishop Konrad Martin asked you to establish an independent Congregation together with a few like-minded women, you were presented with scenes of chaos and suffering in which *"to practice acts of mercy."* With all means available, you cared for destitute orphans and gave them a home, food, education, protection, and emotional support. You also established day-patient care, hospitals, homes for the elderly, and schools. In order to manage such a big workload, new houses were opened — a clear sign of the strengthening of the young Community inside and out. At the time of your death, 1500 Sisters were continuing your work. Were it not for your modesty, you would be very proud of your achievements!

St. Francis was your guide. Just like him, you chose poverty for yourself and connected adoration to acts of mercy. You included the following in the 1865 statutes of the Community: *"Following the example of our holy Father Francis, the Sisters will strive to combine a contemplative and an active life."*

CHAPEL OF PERPETUAL ADORATION IN MISHAWAKA

"He leads — I follow" - into the Future

Your motto *"He leads - I follow"* led you to make the right decisions at the right moments in time, so that your path opened up in front of you where that of others would have ended. Your trust in Divine Leadership caused you to find creative solutions in turbulent and uncertain times that opened the door to the future for your Community. In 1871, Bismarck, Chancellor of the newly-founded German state, joined forces with the liberals in order to repress Catholicism. What followed were the so-called *"May Laws"* of 1873, which severely repressed the Church and Religious Communities and put them under state control. No new members were allowed to join Religious Communities; schools and orphanages were closed down. In these testing times, you concentrated all your efforts on reassuring and strengthening the Sisters by reminding them of the very essence of their vocation: poverty and adoration. Moreover, you were even thinking of new directions in which to lead the Community in those times of its uncertain future.

In 1875, you sent Sisters who were prohibited from working in and around Olpe to found new houses overseas. With the anti-clerical so-called *"Kulturkampf"* raging in Germany, you used the threat to your Community to expand it. To this day, the Provinces in Mishawaka, Indiana, (USA), Colorado Springs, Colorado (USA) and Baybay, Leyte (Philippines) are seeing new Sisters join their Provinces.

During the last years of your life, you were searching for ways to safeguard your Community's existence after your death, particularly in financial terms. Three years before you passed away, in 1902, your Community was added to the Commercial Register as a limited-liability company engaged in caring for children and the sick. The by-laws governing the official registration of trading companies were changed after your death, and in 1995, the Community obtained its current status of a charitable association. In the same year, the Maria Theresia Bonzel Foundation was born. To this day, the association is continuing your work to fulfill the wish you made on your deathbed: *"This love shall prevail!"* Love prevails always. Without love there is nothing.

You achieved many things in your own quiet way. However, your biggest strength was your inner wealth, your immense love for Jesus Christ and the poor in whom He lives on.

"Yes, Olpe has seen a star, a light ignited by God, in the shape of our foundress, our kind-hearted and soulful Mother whose life was all love and suffering" (Sr. Hildegardis Schelle, contemporary).

On the Lighter Side

Sometimes first-graders fear that some lessons are too hard for them. I tried to explain that everyone in our classroom can learn if he listens to the teacher. "If the work is too hard for you, just ask me and I will help you understand what needs to be done". Soon afterwards, while the class was busy with a math test, I noticed Suzy straddling her chair to peek at someone else's paper. (Referring to what I had just explained about doing their own work), I went to Suzy's desk and asked her, "What does Billy have that you don't?" Suzy replied, "The answers."

Then and Now

Dear Mother Maria Theresia, the *"star"* of Olpe, shine a light for us so that we may never lose sight of Heaven, which was *"everything"* to you! You have left traces that lead us to Heaven even today, 150 years after the Community's foundation. We need people like you to guide us through the challenges of the 21st century with their spirituality and experience!

- You strove to become Jesus' likeness and mirrored Him through your prayers and actions. It is only with your help that I can sense what an honor it is to become God's picture. We find our true face not by looking in the mirror but by God's looking at us. Thus He frees us from the pressure of always having to prove to ourselves our right to exist. We can hand ourselves over to a kind God.

- You trusted in the *"benefit"* of faith — a certain placidity when it comes to determining what is possible and what is not because, long before we achieve and earn, we can be sure to possess the most important thing already: our existence confirmed by God.

- You relied on God alone to satisfy our hope and desire for *"more."* He offers the key to relieving our hunger and thirst: our hunger is sated with bread that multiplies when shared; our thirst is quenched by the wine of joy, when we gather around His table.

- Your life of prayer helps me to ponder my strong ties with God and my surrender to His will, so that He may

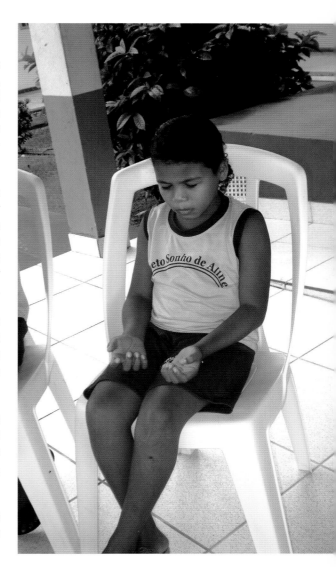

shape me, because He knows better than I what is good for me.

- Your life of stillness helps me to ponder whether I will treat myself to times of *"ear-opening inner silence"* to combat the "deafening inner void" in this noisy world and hear the words that are meant for me.

- Your life of poverty helps me to ponder my relationship with property, the things that I am attached to, those that make me truly happy and others that make me *"look poor."* Whom do I serve? What is my true wealth?

- Your life of mercy helps me to ponder whether I am caring for the needs of others, whether I am looking at instead of looking away, and whether I am spending time and effort on those who need my help here and now.

- Your life of facing the challenges of your time helps me to ponder whether I recognize what is to be done today and whether through my existence I have the courage to point to Him in whose service you placed your life.

- Your life of following helps me to ponder whether I am aware of my own personal vocation and whether I am letting myself be led — like you.

On March 27, 2010, Pope Benedict XVI signed a Decree of Recognition of your heroic virtue. Since then, dear Mother Maria Theresia, you are not simply a *"Servant of God"* anymore, but a *"Venerable Servant of God"*. These are important steps toward your canonization, which was initiated in 1961. What do you think about that? Title and honor do not matter to you where you are now. But maybe it is simply that character trait of yours, your kind modesty, that makes you blessed to us in this world of *"higher, further, faster."*

"Blessed are the poor in spirit, for theirs is the Kingdom of Heaven." (Matthew 5:3)

On the Lighter Side

In August of 1948, I was assigned to teach full time in a first-grade classroom. Little did I know I would be "there" for 50 years. There are just a few "funny" incidents that I recall that happened during my first year of teaching. After two weeks of following a set daily schedule, (including recess at 10:00), little Ruth came to our convent back door on Saturday morning, rang the doorbell, and asked if Sister Robertann could come out and play with her. For a short time the two of us played hopscotch and jumped rope one by one. Two other memories I have of Ruth: after we entered Church for a funeral Mass and got settled in the pews, she counted 6 large lit candles around the casket. Aloud — she looked at me and said, "This is the prettiest thing I've seen happening in a Church." Ruth must have thought I looked hungry; during another Mass, she turned to me and said, "Sister, I brought a nickel for you to buy a treat for yourself."

"He leads - I follow"

MOTHER MARIA THERESIA BONZEL DURING HER VISIT TO NEBRASKA

Chapter II

HOW ALINE BECAME MOTHER MARIA THERESIA — INSIGHTS INTO HER LIFE AND WORK (1830–1905).

BIRTHPLACE

- On September 17, 1830, Regina Christine Wilhelmine, lovingly called *"Aline"*, was born in Olpe.

- She grew up in a wealthy family. Her parents Friedrich Edmund Bonzel, a merchant, and Maria Anna, née Liese, attached great importance to giving Aline and her sister Emilie a well-grounded religious education. Her father died when Aline was seven — a severe disruption to her sheltered, happy upbringing.

- At her First Communion, Aline felt strongly that *"I devote myself to Him who has devoted Himself to me"* and asked: *"O Lord, I am your sacrifice; accept me as such and do not reject me."*

- Aline's mother hoped that she would marry and look after her in her old age. Aline, meanwhile, had other plans. She wanted to join a convent. In 1850, she became a member of the Franciscan lay movement of the Third Order. Her mother at first refused to allow Aline to join a Religious Community. After a long struggle, she finally consented.

- At the age of 29 Aline joined forces with some of her friends with the aim of establishing an association devoted to Perpetual Adoration and to the care and education of orphans and the sick. They formed the Congregation of the *"Sisters of St. Francis"*. During her investiture, she adopted her new name — *"Sister Maria Theresia of the Blessed Sacrament."*

- The sick were also being cared for by a Community of Vincentian nuns, and because of the ensuing conflicts between the two Congregations, the Superior of the *"Sisters of St. Francis"* — Klara Pfänder — made the decision to move their Motherhouse from

Olpe to Salzkotten. The house in Olpe remained, and Sister Maria Theresia took on its administration. Klara Pfänder called many Sisters away from Olpe. This in turn led to tensions, as it was almost impossible to combine care for the needy and Perpetual Adoration in the smaller house in Olpe with fewer Sisters.

On the Lighter Side

During the noon hour, a little boy had fallen on the playground. I went over to see his "problem," and he cried louder. So I told him to pick himself up. He responded: "In the public school kindergarten class, the teacher picked the kids up." I responded: "This is a Catholic school. The Bible says: Get up and walk." He looked at me and answered: "Ok, I'll get up right now" — and off he ran to play!

- Following these conflicts, Bishop Konrad Martin of Paderborn ordered the separation of Olpe and Salzkotten and appointed Sister Maria Theresia as Superior of an independent Congregation in 1863. Sister Maria Theresia became Mother Maria Theresia, and the *"Poor Sisters of St. Francis of*

Perpetual Adoration" was founded as of July 20, 1863. The statutes prepared by Mother Maria Theresia in the name of the *"Poor Sisters of St. Francis of Perpetual Adoration"* and in accordance with the Rule of the Third Order of St. Francis were approved on July 6, 1865. Mother Maria Theresia was subsequently elected Superior General. She was re-elected every three years from 1865 to 1886 when the Community was divided into two Provinces. Thereafter, until her death, she was re-elected every six years.

- The year 1870 saw the outbreak of the Franco-Prussian War. Mother Maria Theresia provided Sisters to care for the wounded. At the same time, renewed conflict emerged in Olpe, this time at the hands of Auxiliary Bishop Freusberg, Superior of the Vincentian Sisters, who saw the Franciscans as competitors and wanted to stop them from caring for the sick. After a long tug-of-war, Mother Maria Theresia finally obtained the permission of the State for her Community to continue with its work in this field.

MÜLHEIM/MÖHNE

NOVICES IN MÜLHEIM

permission to care for the sick seemed even more important, as from then on, Religious Communities were allowed to work in this one field only.

- Mother Maria Theresia secured the longevity of her Community through the establishment of new houses in North America. The year 1875 saw the arrival of the first Sisters in Lafayette, Indiana, where they immediately started teaching and caring for the sick. New houses were founded and new postulants invested. While the Community in Germany fought for permission to do any work at all, the American houses were developing rapidly. Mother Maria Theresia kept in contact with her Sisters overseas through the regular exchange of letters. Moreover, she visited her Sisters in America three times, despite her failing health and the stressful journey.

- The *"Kulturkampf"* took place from 1871 until 1878 between the Catholic Church under Pope Pius IX and the Kingdom of Prussia; later — between the former and the newly united German Empire under Chancellor Bismarck. The anti-clerical reaction it embodied led to far-reaching consequences, restrictions, and prohibitions for the Church and its Religious Communities, and finally to a separation of Church and State. In the light of these developments, Mother Maria Theresia's fight for official

- State sanctions against the Church were relaxed around 1880, as a result of which new postulants could be invested in Olpe and new houses founded. Yet again the old tensions with Auxiliary Bishop Freusberg flared up — his aim was still to keep the Franciscan Sisters from carrying out healthcare work, a wish that was eventually granted in 1884 through an Episcopal decree. Subsequently, in 1885, some of the

Aline wants to know

And what is the black ring for?

The black ring, made from the fruit of the Brazilian Tucumã palm tree, is a symbol of the Franciscan's wish to care especially for the poor.

Sisters moved to Mülheim, where the novitiate was being set up. The Sisters only returned to the Motherhouse in Olpe ten years later. During this time, around 600 novices had prepared for life in the Community.

- The return of the novitiate to Olpe required the construction of a larger Motherhouse which was inaugurated in 1895. Once again the Sisters were allowed to care for the sick; in addition, Sisters were sent to teach in various schools. New houses were established, too, among them St. Mary Hospital on Mt. Venus in Bonn. The hospital enjoyed a very good reputation. In all, 110 houses were founded in Germany and overseas under Mother Maria Theresia.

- Her life and work were finally being honored publicly. In 1897 she received a Decree of Praise and Commendation for her Community, and in 1900 Emperor Wilhelm II awarded her a Red-Cross Medal for the outstanding work of her Community. Two months before her passing, her Community was admitted to the First Order of St. Francis, which meant that it now enjoyed the same privileges as other Franciscan Orders.

- Three years prior to her death, Mother Maria Theresia put all her efforts into safeguarding her Community's future. She protected her association's assets through civil law, and in 1902, it was added to the Commercial Register as a limited-liability company engaged in caring for children and the sick.

- The last years of her life were *"a chronicle of suffering"* (Lothar Hardick,OFM). She suffered heart attacks and ever more frequent physical weakness. Yet still she exhibited joy and placidity, and remained a fountain of solace and care for her Sisters. She left them the following legacy: *"I have loved you all without exception, and this love shall prevail!"* Her last words on her deathbed were: *"Patience! Patience! Come soon my Savior!"*

- Mother Maria Theresia died on February 6, 1905.

He led — she followed, carried by God. She followed Him home.

"He Leads - I Follow"

POST CARD SHOWING THE FIRST MOTHERHOUSE IN OLPE

CHAPTER III

ONLY THROUGH CHANGE CAN THERE BE CONTINUITY — LIFE IN THE COMMUNITY AFTER MOTHER MARIA THERESIA'S DEATH

MOTHER PAULA THOMAS, 2ND SUPERIOR GENERAL

With the help of our chronicles, this overview attempts to chart the development of our Community from Mother Maria Theresia's death to today.

When Mother Maria Theresia died, the Community was 42 years old. The foundress's death was a significant event in the Sisters' lives. The election of a new Superior General was the first necessary step toward the Community's ongoing development. As early as May 25, 1905, the role was taken on by Sister Paula Thomas. On the same day the foundation stone of the new novitiate was laid — the advent of another change. Until then, the novitiate had had its home in Mülheim/Möhne. Over 600 Sisters had been educated there.

The following years were characterized by the establishment of numerous new houses and the joining of new members. The mourning of the loss of Mother Maria Theresia was somewhat brightened up by Mother Paula's loving but firm leadership.

The outbreak of the First World War put the Sisters in a precarious situation. At first 15 Sisters were called to the front in Lüttich to look after the wounded. More Sisters followed. They worked not only on the western but also on the eastern front, as far afield as Croatia and Romania. In all, 40 Sisters worked in military hospitals during the war.

Mother Paula died on December 11, 1914, completely unexpectedly. An Olpe newspaper commented:

"Thanks to her loving leadership, the association grew from 65 houses with 870 Sisters to 91 houses with 1100 Sisters, who work in healthcare and education."

The next chapter took place two years later. Because of the war the American Sisters could not participate. Mother Verena Schulte was elected General Superior.

Mother Verena was to be in this position for 31 years. It is thanks to her leadership that the Community grew further. She was also responsible for the courageous and future-focused rebuilding of existing houses and the establishment of new ones after the two World Wars.

As early as 1919 the Community-owned premises on Mt. Kimicker were expanded through the purchase of more land in order to build a new Motherhouse. It would be 44 years before this plan was realized.

Besides looking after children in St. Joseph's House, in 1921 the Sisters began handing out soup as breakfast to malnourished children before school.

The project was funded by an industrialist from the city of Olpe. Around 60 children were thus provided with breakfast for two months. After that, it was to be the turn of other needy children. Two years later, the Sisters were helping out in a soup kitchen that had been set up by the city of Olpe for citizens in need. Famine, price increases and high inflation (a loaf of bread back then cost 1 trillion 200 billion Marks) forced limitations on the Sisters and required the development of creative solutions in order to help those in need.

Despite all adversity, increasing numbers of Sisters took exams in healthcare, child education, home economics, social welfare and teaching after the First World War.

On January 31, 1931, the Religious Community was officially recognized as a Congregation of Papal Right. At the same time, demands were made that Provinces should be established in Germany as well as the United States, as the number of Sisters had hugely increased.

MOTHER VERENA SCHULTE, 3RD GENERAL SUPERIOR

In Germany the *"Province of the Sacred Heart of Jesus"* and the *"Province of the Holy Family"* were created, with 26 and 56 houses, respectively. The two Provinces consisted of 1408 Sisters in Perpetual Vows, 108 novices, and 57 postulants.

At the same time the *"Immaculate Heart of Mary"* and *"St. Joseph"* Provinces were formed in the US with 43 and 37 houses, respectively, with 999 Sisters in Perpetual Vows, 33 novices and 53 postulants.

Each Province developed its own character according to its individual cultural conditions.

Aline wants to know

Do you wear your dress at night?

Of course not. I sleep in a nightgown or pajamas, just like you. My habit simply shows that women who wear it are religious Sisters. Every Community has its own dress – in Germany and the US it is brown; in the Philippines it is white.

It is noteworthy that many German Sisters continued to live in the America convents and supported their work.

The terrifying consequences of National Socialism in Germany also touched the Sisters' lives. Kindergartens were closed and Sisters were replaced by state employees. These years were characterized by continuing dissolutions. Children's homes, needle-work schools, home-economics courses and, eventually, schools, were badly affected. The Community was forced to be flexible. The Sisters had to comply, since acting or protesting would have been life-threatening.

Just like the German populace as a whole, our Sisters were confronted with all kinds of emergency and fearful situations unimaginable. Schools and civilian hospitals were turned into military hospitals.

Thirty-three Sisters lost their lives in bombing raids. Contact with the American Sisters had ceased completely, so no General Chapter could take place and Mother Verena remained in office. Staying and changing? Yes, through facing new challenges whose solution was not guaranteed.

Through it all, new Sisters were invested into the Community in Germany as well as in the US. There were no signs of resignation to be found anywhere in the chronicles, only signs of worry, fear and consternation.

After the war, our Community found itself amidst ruins. And yet signs were pointing towards a new beginning. Schools and other institutions led and shaped by the Sisters were rebuilt.

Finally, contact with the American Sisters was possible again. There was great joy over this renewed

On the Lighter Side

One day as I was opening the back door of the convent, one of my students was passing by the house and he asked: "Sister, do you live in that big convent?" I responded, "Yes, I do." "So where does Sister James live?" he asked. I answered, "Sister James (the Principal) lives here, too." Zach was stunned and expressed himself excitedly, "Wow, all my life I never heard of anyone living with their boss."

LAYING OF THE FOUNDATION STONE FOR A NEW OPERATING THEATRE AT ST. MARY'S HOSPITAL, BONN, AFTER THE WAR

feeling of belonging, and also over the many parcels sent from America, which greatly relieved the food shortages the children at St. Joseph's House and the Sisters were experiencing.

In 1947 Mother Verena, by then 84 years old, could finally welcome the American delegates at the General Chapter and pass on her office to Mother Fabiana Schulte.

Mother Fabiana actively supported the reconstruction and establishment of new houses. Yet during her term in office the number of new members decreased rapidly. As early as 1953 the German General Superiors met at a conference to discuss the issue. Not all participants saw the urgency that this problem demanded as clearly as Mother Fabiana. Today we might question the dissolution of smaller convents for the benefit of the bigger institutions, but a clear decision was reached in the spirit of *"continuity through change."* Mother Fabiana's wisdom was also manifest in the founding of new institutions, such as a preparatory school for healthcare professions in Olpe in 1958.

MOTHER FABIANA SCHULTE,
4TH GENERAL SUPERIOR

The inter-German border separating East and West Germany was an additional burden on the Community, especially when over time this border became ever more impermeable and led to divisions. Young women in the Russian sector were looking to join our Community. Even if they managed to cross the border, it would be impossible for them to return and work in the Russian sector. One of our Sisters, Sr. Sigrada Witte, had crossed the border *"illegally"* in 1951 on foot when she was found dead. The official report stated *"death by heat stroke."* However, everything pointed to her having been shot. At that time, everyone had to keep quiet. It was only after re-unification that the truth surfaced.

MEMORIAL STONE ON THE FORMER
INTER-GERMAN BORDER IN HÖTENSLEBEN

Our concerns about the declining number of new Sisters were shared by all Communities in East Germany. That is why we decided, once legally possible, to open a second novitiate, first in Lengenfeld-unterm-Stein and later in Oschersleben, both in Thuringia, a province in the former East Germany. Early 1961, in the middle of the Cold War, Sr. Laurentiana Antpöhler offered herself to take on the education of the novices and the tasks of Regional Superior in Oschersleben, whose consequences no one could predict.

On September 18, 1961, Archbishop Cardinal Jaeger of Paderborn initiated the beatification process of the Community's founder, Mother Maria Theresia Bonzel. All Sisters rejoiced at the news. No one would have guessed back then that this process would still be on-going 50 years later.

Despite a lack of new members the Sisters decided to go one step further. In August 1963, a few days after the Community's centenary, five Sisters were sent to Brazil as missionaries. With huge personal effort they have been looking after the poor

CARDINAL LORENZ JAEGER, ARCHBISHOP OF PADERBORN, OPENS THE PROCESS OF BEATIFICATION FOR MOTHER MARIA THERESIA BONZEL IN 1963

for decades. In partnership with the young Brazilian Sisters, the last few years have seen the creation of the *"Sonho de Aline"* project for children.

Due to various circumstances, the Motherhouse on Mt. Kimicker by Olpe had to be built. The architect Hans Schilling (Cologne) designed the new complex in such a way that not only does it fit into the convent's natural surroundings; but also by grouping the various buildings around the church, he accentuated the Community's very center and source of life, as well as spiritual and charitable activities.

The declining number of new members and the aging of the other Sisters remained a big challenge. However, the Sisters continued to work in the institutions with great dedication, which made it very painful when the convents' involvement had to be withdrawn from some

On the Lighter Side

Mike must have been having a bad day. He became unruly and told me he didn't like all the work he had to do in school. Mike decided he would end his problems by speaking <u>loud and clear</u>,

BLESSING OF THE NEW MOTHERHOUSE CORNERSTONE

"My dad gets home at 4:00. I'm going to meet him at the door and tell him to get his gun and go to school to shoot you, teacher." I responded, "I will be hiding under my desk, so it won't take long to find me." Sure enough, his dad came to my classroom about 4:00 (without a gun – but he brought his son)! Both apologized and Mike learned his lesson.

49

of them. This situation resulted in the decision to unite the two German Provinces into one. Thus, in 1993, St. Elizabeth of Thuringia Province was created.

Another decision concerned the institutions themselves in which our Sisters had not held any leading positions for some time. Since 1983, when the limited-liability company's management was extended, knowledgeable business economists have been acting as company directors and advising the Sisters.

The Maria Theresia Bonzel Foundation, established in 1995, replaced the limited-liability company as shareholder of the *"Charitable Association of the Franciscans of Olpe."* While the foundation acted as shareholder, the limited-liability company remained in charge of the economic management of the association.

Sisters are still present on the charitable association's Board of Directors and take part in decision-making processes. Furthermore, structures were created that instilled our foundress's Christian values and spirit into today's thoughts and actions.

"Only through change can there be continuity." Many changes come about in small steps. Through the establishment of smaller convents, first in Bonn and then in Olpe, the Sisters have been trying to regain access to people's lives. The few younger Sisters use their creativity and flexibility to create opportunities to fulfill our task — "to adore and to work in the spirit of mercy" – in today's world.

A description of the many more important and interesting developments would go beyond the scope of this commemorative booklet. Yet I want to point out one more discovery. Our annalist wrote in 1932 that one of Mother Maria Theresia Bonzel's favorite citations was "per crucem ad lucem." (through the cross to light)

I would like to attach this phrase to our most familiar quote:

"HE leads. I follow. — Per crucem ad lucem."

Sr. Magdalena Krol

Something amusing from the Chronicles

HELPING HANDS IN THE CAFÉ

October 27, 1958: Tonight saw a great commotion in the house. Sister Everildis was not in her room. We searched the whole house top to bottom, but she was nowhere to be found. She has been a bit confused for some time, and often does not realize what she is doing. Several Sisters were sent out to look for her in the city but every single one returned without her. We searched the whole garden with torches, but without success. So we notified the police, and two officers in a car searched the town high and low. After three hours without finding her we became very worried. Where could the poor, elderly Sister be? Perhaps she had collapsed outside? Many a prayer was offered up to St. Anthony. What else could we do? We were supposed to be celebrating our jubilarians' birthdays the next day! The whole house had been searched at least three times. Suddenly, it must have been after 10 p.m., the upper floor was filled with cries of joy. Our dear Sister Everildis had been found. She was fast asleep in Sister Consolata's bed.

August 15, 1971: This Sunday, Ascension Day, ended in a bull chase. We were enjoying each others' company after dinner when we got news that our 12 bulls were on the loose. Many Sisters ran outside and toward the woods. After a few minutes, the whole convent was on its feet. The new fence that had only recently been erected on the edge of the woods had been cut, allowing the bulls to escape. Now we had to look for them. After a while we saw the first escapees grazing with other livestock in a different meadow. The remaining bulls were found in yet another one. Only one bull was roaming the woods. It took us some time to round him up and get him back to the others. Night had fallen when we finally made our way home. Two Jesuit Brothers who were spending their vacation with us had also taken part in the chase. In the Motherhouse everyone was waiting for us. Some thought that our bulls had been stolen; others had called on St. Anthony for help. When word got around that we had retrieved all the animals, everybody rejoiced. Some Sisters returned with their tights in tatters. As a reward we had an ice-cream party afterwards. The next morning our men went to fetch the bulls and led them calmly through the woods. Once they were back in their meadow, some of them started to bellow loudly – they must have been happy to be back home!

"For He has sent you out into the world to attest to His voice through words and deeds."

(St. Francis)

THE ANIMALS TAKE A BREAK…

"HE LEADS - I FOLLOW"

55

INTER-GERMAN BORDER IN HÖTENSLEBEN, STATE OF SAXONY-ANHALT

CHAPTER IV

"WE WERE LIKE THOSE WHO DREAMED" — LIFE IN A THURINGIAN CONVENT AFTER GERMAN RE-UNIFICATION IN 1989

When the Lord restored
the fortunes of Zion,
we were like those who dreamed.
Our mouths were filled with laughter,
our tongues with songs of joy.
Then it was said among the nations:
"The Lord has done
great things for them."

(Psalm 126, 1-2)

Sr. Laurentiana Antpöhler
wrote the following letter
in a convent located inside
the 3-mile exclusion zone
on the inter-German border
in Thuringia:

GDR-5701 Lengenfeld-unterm-Stein,
10. 11. 1989

Dear Sister Xaveria,
Dear Sisters!

The events in our country today are moving the other Sisters and me to such an extent that I have decided to share our experiences with you in this impromptu report.

Since the early hours of the morning there has been only one topic in this country, in the town and in our house. The borders are open. The exclusion zone and protective strip have disappeared. We cannot grasp its immensity; it is unbelievable. The first West German car passed through the village around noon. It is all so exciting, exhausting, liberating. The first young people have set off toward the border crossing in their cars carrying only their I.D. cards — they went to take a look, perhaps to see some of their relatives on the other side, and to return. At least that is what we hope. Everything has been set in motion — excitedly but in a civilized way. The people work during the day and at night they are on the streets or in the churches; there is a great solidarity between Christians and non-Christians. We all share the same concern: the hope for a radical change.

You can watch what is happening on television. But East German television, our news programs especially, has become more interesting than yours. The same is true for our newspapers; they have become readable, even interesting. Nothing is being glossed over anymore; lies are being uncovered and acknowledged. Everyone says what he

On the Lighter Side

As I was supervising the playground, Tommy followed me around. He had noticed a gold band on my ring finger and asked if I was married. I responded "Yes, Sisters are sometimes called 'Brides of Jesus'. So he asked, "Well, are you the bride of the one who lives there (pointing to the priest's house) or the one who lives over there?" (pointing to the Church. Needless to say, I explained the whole idea in our next religion class.

59

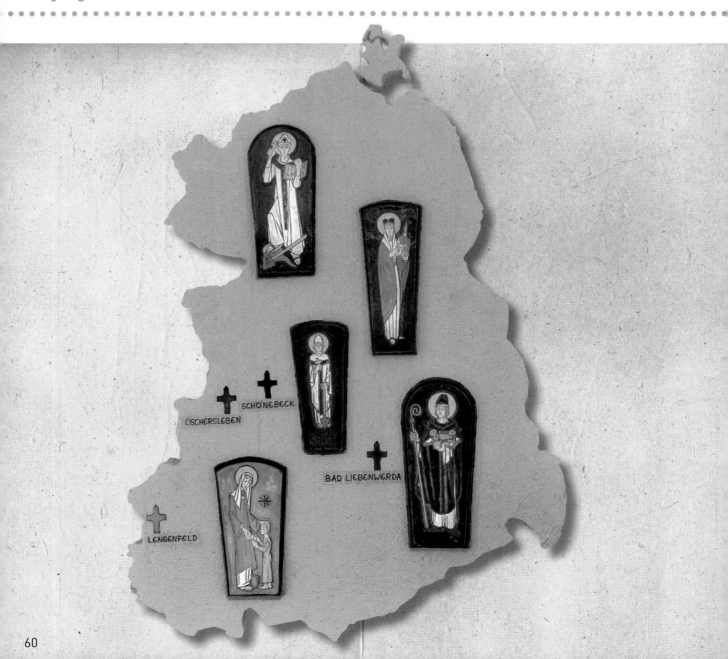

OSCHERSLEBEN

SCHÖNEBECK

BAD LIEBENWERDA

LENGENFELD

thinks. What happened so publicly on Berlin's Alexanderplatz had been taking place in every city, town and village. The ecumenical services conducted in Leipzig and Berlin were copied by all churches in the German Democratic Republic.

Last Monday I took part in an ecumenical service for peace in Oschersleben. It started at 7 p.m.; around 8.20 all the participants left the church carrying candles and singing "Lord, give us Your peace." In silence we walked through the town. All the seats in the big church had been taken by 6 p.m. Everyone came — Christians and non-Christians — possibly more non-baptized than baptized. The Catholic and Evangelical priests led the service very well. A few young people were singing catchy peace songs, accompanied by a guitar. A selection from the Prophet Amos was guiding the way then and today, sounding as fresh and current as never before. People laughed and clapped before breaking into a song of peace. Father Krause kept repeating: "The Holy Spirit blows where He wills." We were informed of the events in Dresden's opera house, and of a New Forum that had been created in Oschersleben, in between singing and prayers. After half an hour the structure changed slightly. Two microphones installed in the aisles gave all those present the opportunity to present their pleas, intercessions, wishes and complaints, which were answered with a kyrie eleison. Even the mayor, a member of the Socialist Unity Party, stepped up to the microphone. He acknowledged that the party had made many mistakes, but asked everyone for the chance of a new beginning together. The applause he received showed many people's approval. He even walked through town with us. The reaction to the mayor's words proved that he was and is a good man, who will presumably remain in office. The party has started "cleaning up" its ranks. Most of the leading officials in charge of towns, companies, districts and regions will be replaced.

When I rang the department responsible for the churches in Berlin, I was told that no one was working there today, as everything was just so exciting. Mixed in with this joy, however, were concerns about the future — many people had already decided to leave the country for good. This has left us with many gaps in numerous areas of the economy, and in social institutions, that are impossible to fill.

The events in our country show the subliminal that has been alive all the time and the suffering that was endured. During parents' evening at a school the parents were told that from now on political-education classes would be cancelled. Religious holidays are to be recognized once more, and the turnpikes on the roads to the towns in the exclusion zone and protective strip are to disappear.

Membership in the youth arm of the party is to be voluntary.

Citizens are celebrating these sudden and unbelievable events with family parties, wine and champagne. A small shop sold 20 bottles of champagne today. Even our priest will open a bottle with his housekeeper and her family — it has lain unopened for 11 years. When the priest moved to Lengenfeld in the middle of the exclusion zone 11 years ago, he bought the champagne in the hope that one day he might celebrate freedom. He never gave up hope.

All of the Sisters spent time together tonight to talk about the current events and make possible travel plans, particularly to the Motherhouse. We will soon be applying for visas for all of the Sisters.

Today, tomorrow and on Sunday many people from the village will be going to Duderstadt, just on the other side of the

Aline wants to know

Why did you decide to become a nun?

Through my prayers and my questions regarding God and Jesus Christ, I one day felt that I wanted to live as a religious Sister. I joined the Franciscans because the life of St. Francis appealed to me very much.

ROAD NEAR LENGENFELD-UNTERM-STEIN, THURINGIA

On the Lighter Side

Our Principal was setting up a classroom for an upcoming pre-school class. On the PA system she asked the students if anyone had nice toys stored in the basement. She would appreciate them, if they were not being used at home anymore. Suzie had heard that message before, so she said to me, "I told my mom about it, but she said: 'I'm saving them for when I become a grandma'." So the topic ended there – except for an hour later. Bobby came to me and whispered in my ear, "I don't want to embarrass you or hurt your feelings, Sister, but are you a grandma yet?" My only reply was "<u>NOT YET.</u>" (I knew he would learn later what that's all about).

border, to have a look around. I hope that after this rush prudence will return.

I can see God's work in all of these events. We entrust the future to His leadership. These days, closeness to God can be felt stronger than before; it is a time of God and the Church. People's awareness of the Church and the churches is more pronounced than ever. Spontaneous words of thanks during services are proof of this. What Cardinal Newman said during a prayer remains true:

O Lord, in these times of distress
Christ's cause seems in mortal agony.
And yet - never was Christ mightier
On earth;
Never was his coming clearer;
Never his closeness more tangible;
Never his service more ambrosial
Than now.
So let us pray on earth
At this moment
In between storms:
O Lord, you can light up the darkness,
You alone can do it!

I feel connected with you
through this belief.
The Sisters and I send you
our warmest regards.

Your

Sister M. Lauréntiana

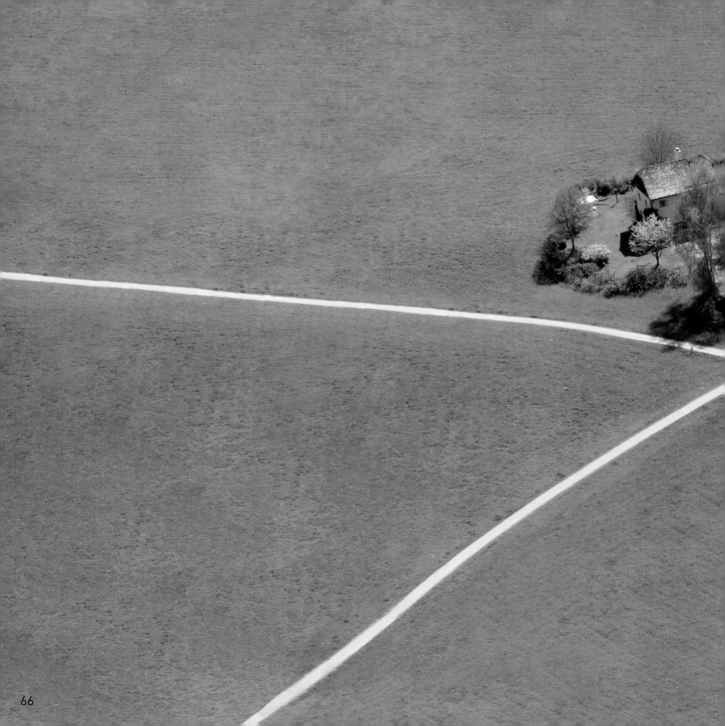

"HE LEADS - I FOLLOW"

*FIRST MOTHERHOUSE IN
THE CENTER OF OLPE*

MUTTERHAUS

FÜR LIEFERANTEN

HOSTIENBÄCKEREI

CHAPTER V — WELCOME TO THE MOTHERHOUSE

Although I am called the Motherhouse, there are actually no mothers living inside me. That might seem a little confusing. I am the first, the original house of the Franciscan Sisters of Olpe. All the other houses that have been created are my daughters. Perhaps you are now thinking: *"You don't look that old!"* You are right. I have only been looking this way for the last 50 years. In the olden days my home was next to the train station in Olpe, and I looked completely different — my style was called neo-Gothic. It was very popular in the late 19th century. For many years my shape was constantly changing in order to meet all the needs of the Community.

My rooms were filled with life from the very first day. Sometimes I felt like a girls' boarding school, particularly during the arrival of up to 50 postulants from April to October. I could not help but smile when the older, venerable Sisters were trying to teach the exuberant youngsters some *"monasterial discipline."*

"One does not behave like this, young lady!" was one of the phrases I heard all too often. Well, I have to admit that life does not work without rules. However, as the Motherhouse, I closed my eyes and ears and did not meddle. For me it was a great pleasure to see the Sisters return, either for the profession of their vows or to celebrate the anniversary thereof.

Aline wants to know

Do you also eat Nutella for breakfast?

Usually not. Most Sisters find Nutella simply too sweet. We eat jam instead.

One of my other wings — does *"guardian angel"* not spring to mind? — was inhabited by many orphans. I looked after them with my big protective walls. Joy, suffering, tenderness, but every now and then, incomprehensible strictness, were all at home here.

My heartbeat could be heard at the place of Perpetual Adoration. Carried by Christ's lasting Presence, the Sisters spent day and night here, bringing with them their thanks, pleas, worries and joys. They returned to their daily tasks with renewed strength, courage, solace, and the feeling that Someone was listening.

Naturally, the most significant period of my life was when Mother Maria Theresia lived inside me. Every encounter and every talk has become deeply engraved in my walls.

This connection with Mother Maria Theresia goes so deep that I managed to carry the spirit of these experiences with me when I took on my current shape. For this I am thankful to Him who still lives in my heart: Jesus Christ. After Mother Maria Theresia's death, I looked out onto her burial chapel and this was how we remained close, a closeness that lasts to this day.

Of course not all has been well and good for me all the time. I have survived two wars — the last one not without wounds and injuries. Yet the Sisters looked after me so well that soon enough I was able to give them and the children a home once more.

When in the 1960s I was told that my structure had become weak and that new laws had been introduced regarding the care of orphans, and that any attempts at my beautification would be in vain, I was as shocked and frightened as my daughters. Furthermore, I was going to be tightly enclosed by roads — the little pond next door was to become a big lake, which meant a change to the routing and configuration of the roads in Olpe. Demolition? Reconstruction? Would I be able to remain the same inside despite my new appearance? But *"to live is to change"*, and regarding myself there were many important reasons for these changes.

What did not change was my purpose. I am still the center of our widely-dispersed Community. I am the seat of the Generalate and the General Superior

WINTERTIME IN THE FIRST MOTHERHOUSE

lives and works here, too. Here, close to Mother Maria Theresia's grave, we keep everything that illustrates our history. I am even home to the German Province's administrative body.

Moreover, I always keep my doors open for my daughters. Meeting days, exercises, weekends, seminars and other events take place here. Every four years delegated Sisters from the German Province meet at the Provincial Chapter. They discuss important issues, make decisions, and elect a new Provincial Leadership.

On the Lighter Side

In the classroom I always stressed how important it is to do your best work and behave — follow the rules. This is important in all the years you are in school, not just in first grade! When you get older and want a job, or you want to go to Notre Dame or IU for college, someone will call the school office to find out if you did your class work on time, all your homework — and if you behaved. Then I added: If you don't believe this, I can prove it to you. I put report cards in the Principal's office 40 years ago and they are still there. Overwhelmed with this news, Danny smacked his forehead and said, "Golly, 40 years ago! It's a good thing you're so healthy or you would have been dead a long time ago!"

Sr. Danielis

THE SISTERS' REFECTORY IN THE MOTHERHOUSE

I also feel that we are an International Community. Every six years Sisters from the four Provinces – Eastern USA, Western USA, Philippines, and Germany which includes the mission in Brazil — meet at the General Chapter. Important matters are discussed and a new General Leadership is elected. When Sisters arrive for these international meetings, there is always such an exciting and bilingual buzz. It is then that I realize than I am indeed the *"mother of many."*

SISTERS IN THE AUDITORIUM

Open doors and an open heart are most important to me. Jesus Christ, who lives inside me, helps me keep my heart open, as does the fact that even after 150 years the Sisters remain in contact with Him through their hours of adoration. This is how the heartbeat comes to life; not only for our Sisters but also for others. Perpetual Adoration is the real *"center of power."*

Through their work and hospitality, the Sisters, along with all the employees who live inside me, help me keep my doors open. We provide many different groups of people with space for seminars, retreats, visits and holiday activities. My green surroundings, a generous choice of rooms, the silence, and the opportunities for prayer and participation in the Eucharist, are inspiring and inviting.

There is much to be seen and discovered inside me. I was built from 1963 to 1967 by an architect called Schilling from Cologne. I believe that those who know his name will expect an interesting building. And this is indeed what I am: extensive, attractive, everything under one roof. Alas, after 50 years I may have become a little too big, but changes are difficult to make.

What interests my visitors most, though, is something completely different. Hidden inside me is a Host Bakery. People of all ages enjoy seeing how the Hosts for Holy Mass are actually made — bread that becomes the Bread of Life.

Thus I see myself as a sort of food — food for thought. Up here on Mt. Kimicker, I am here primarily for my daughters, but also for everyone who wants to be my guest for whatever reason. This is what I have told the Superior General, Sr. Magdalena, today, so she can pass it on to you.

Once again: Welcome to the Motherhouse!

WELCOME TO THE COFFEE SHOP!

"HE LEADS - I FOLLOW"

Being a mouse on the wall of
the Motherhouse

Chapter VI

Being a fly on the wall of the Motherhouse — In place of an interview

I climb up the last bit of steep hill to the Motherhouse. Today I am meeting Sister Magdalena, the General Superior, on the occasion of the Community's anniversary. On the way to the entrance I pass Mr. Teusch. He works with the janitor, and is in charge of driving the Sisters on all the automobile journeys that are organized by Sister Danielis. When I ask him whether Sister Magdalena is at home, he smiles and answers: *"Yes, she's just arrived in her car."* I ring the doorbell, the door-opener buzzes.

I lean against the heavy door and 11 yards of corridor open up in front of me. When I tell Ms. Lütticke that I have an appointment with Sister Magdalena, she says that I will find her in her office on the second floor. So I continue walking through the long corridor. A door to my right is open. I curiously peek inside and see Sister Regina, who is in the process of lovingly preparing the room for a meeting. Homemade cookies and a bunch of fresh rhododendrons from the convent's park adorn the table. I carry on, push down the huge

ENTRANCE

WE PRIDE OURSELVES ON HOSPITALITY

door handle in the shape of an angel and find myself in a big square in the middle of the house. While I marvel at the immensity of the space, I notice laughter and music — something seems to be going on here today. The sounds lead me to the refectory. I am being greeted in several languages, as it turns out that jubilarians from Brazil, the US, and the Philippines are in the house. Sister Veronika, who shares a home with other Sisters in the centre of Olpe, is holding her saxophone in front of her, while Sister Maria José from Brazil re-positions her guitar. The Sisters learning a dance routine are from the Philippines. Their habits have been transformed into dance dresses with the help of colorful shawls. I wish them all the best and notice that I have missed the staircase that leads to the upper floors. I retrace my steps and climb up the

spiral staircase — once again I am faced with a long corridor. Sister Magdalena's office must be somewhere around here. I walk slowly to read the signs on the doors and almost collide with Sister Gertraud, who is leaving one of the rooms in a hurry. She greets me affectionately, as usual. What would you imagine the Province's treasurer to be like? Strict, I am sure. Sister Getraud is completely different. She is a businesswoman body and soul, looks after the Sisters' pensions, and is in charge of the running costs and finances of the entire German Province. Yet she is a very kind person — she used to train nurses, and taught them the importance of keeping an eye on everything that is going on in the hospital ward. She informs me that Sister Magdalena is in the adoration chapel for prayers and rest. The shortest way there is down the staircase. I lope

DOOR KNOB ON THE CRYPT'S DOOR

"MOTHER MARIA THERESIA TOOK THIS SUITCASE TO AMERICA. PLEASE RETAIN!"

down the steps and pause in front of a door leading to the next floor. Is this really where the chapel is? It is a bit confusing with five floors. It smells of fresh pastries. I take a few steps and bump into Sister Gerlinde. No, this is not the chapel but the Host Bakery. I took one flight of stairs too many. Sister Gerlinde bakes Hosts for 200 other communities. For reasons of hygiene I am not allowed into the bakery proper, but can still marvel at the old Host molds from a safe distance. I am beginning to feel like Sherlock Holmes. I have found many features of the Community already, but am still looking for my interviewee.

Aline wants to know

Do you pray all the time?

Not all the time. But I try not to forget that God is always here and listening, and that Jesus remains by my side.

Every Sister takes part in joint prayers: the Morning Prayer (Lauds), the Noon Prayer, the Evening Prayer (Vespers), and the end-of-the-day Prayer (Compline), and of course every day the Holy Mass.

In addition, every Sister prays alone for one hour.

So I climb up the stairs again and turn right. The hallway lights up, thanks to the windows facing onto the pretty courtyard. I look down and see the well-looked-after fish pond — but no, I must not daydream but work. I walk on and finally see the sign that says "Adoration Chapel." This is where I find Sister Magdalena praying together with the Sister "on duty." In addition to their charitable work the Sisters have dedicated themselves to Perpetual Adoration, where every Sister takes a "turn." Although adoration only takes place in Olpe from 11 a.m. to 8 p.m., round-the-clock adoration is guaranteed through the other Provinces in different countries because of the time difference. I bow in front of the magnificent monstrance, which dates from Mother Maria Theresia's time. Sister Madgalena indicates that she will come with me. We decide to delve back into the past to find out more about life in the Motherhouse and as General Superior. Sister Magdalena suggests that we visit Mother Maria Theresia's memorial room. We take another flight of stairs down, and walk through the crypt. The silence gives this room a special atmosphere.

I turn a door knob in the shape of a snake, which reminds me of the movie "The Name of the Rose." I cannot see Sean Connery though ... must not get lost in my imagination! We climb another set of stairs, cross the vestry and arrive at the memorial room. The mosaic window looks pretty and gives the room a lot of light. Many of Mother

Maria Theresia's objects are being kept here — e.g. the child's chair on which she used to rest her legs, her rosary, a tiny Bible, some of her letters, and the penitence belt she hardly ever used. Sister Magdalena puts my mind at rest when she says that penitential discipline rituals neither were nor are common practice in the Community.

I ask Sister Magdalena how many General Superiors there were before her. She points to the Wall behind me: *"If I am counting right, I am the ninth."* A little line below the photographs states the years in office of each General Superior. I notice that Mother Verena Schulte, the third General Superior, had remained in office for a very long time. Normally the Superior is elected for a 6-year term and can be re-elected once. However, Mother Verena Schulte was in office from 1916 to 1947 — 31 years! *"This is due to the two World Wars. Her term was extended because the American Sisters could not attend the General Chapter in Germany,"* Sister Magdalena explains. Now my eye is caught by a determined-looking Sister — Francesco Brüggemann, the fifth General Superior. The dates below her photograph tell me that she must have been the one who planned the construction of the current Motherhouse, in which I had got lost so many times today. I mention that Sister Francesco has a bit of a stern expression.

DANKE

DANKE

DA
19

M. R. 1985

In Dankbarkeit

M.B.   **1987**

In dankbarer Erinnerung
gewidmet der Ordensstifterin
unserer guten Mutter
Maria Theresia Bonzel
bei Hilfe in großer Wassernot
NeunKirchen   1947
St. Franziskus - Krankenhaus

D
A

DANKE!
UTTER M. THERESIA
HAT GEHOLFEN
M. M. 1979

Mo

In großer
Donkbarkeit
S.J.   1977

KE
5
B. E.

Maraming Salamat
Mother Maria Theresia

THE BEBAS FAMILY
CAVITE CITY, PHILIPPINES
YEAR 2000

Damo nga Salamat

MOTHER THERESIA BONZEL, OSF

S E C
Baybay Leyte, Philippines
2002

KE

ER FÜHRT-ICH GEHE
DANKE
2002

Danke
Juni 2003

k 'You

aria Theresia

gie Family
2, 1999
da U.S.A.

DANKE
MUTTER
M-THERESIA

97

Being a mouse on the wall of the Motherhouse - will have you experiencing a typically Olpe kind of "woman power"!

In a religion class, I tried to explain to the first graders the idea of making a promise. First, I used very simple examples they could understand: cleaning their bedroom, picking up clothes, etc. Then I added, "Your mom and dad make promises. Sisters make promises also. I promised to be a Sister forever – and to wear brown forever." A few weeks later, Michael Jordan decided to retire from basketball. So in class one day, I said: "Well, I better go to Chicago and help the Bulls. Now that Jordan won't be there, they will need help so they will keep on winning." Immediately, a little boy came to my desk and excitedly said, "Sister, you can't go to Chicago to help the Bulls; they wear red, and you promised to wear brown forever!"

Sister Magdalena chuckles: *"When I first decided to take a look around the convent in Oschersleben, I asked about the dress code. I was told that it was OK to just wear my everyday clothes, jeans, to start with. You cannot imagine the look on Sister Francesco's face when she first saw me!"* A picture of Mary has a special place on the wall on the left-hand side —

it survived a fire in Mother Maria Theresia's family home. We are short of time, Sister Magdalena has another appointment — the singing and dancing Sisters are waiting for her. We climb and descend another few flights of stairs. Sister Magdalena has to open some doors with her master key, and we turn a few more door knobs in the shape of mystical characters and

symbols. I spot the cross from the first oratory in 1860 which the Sisters had been given, go through the chapel with the very tall tower where Mass is celebrated regularly, curiously inspect the suitcase made of willow branches in the memorial room which Mother Maria Theresia took with her to America more than 100 years ago, and even take a peek at her bedroom.

No matter where one goes in the Motherhouse, one is constantly encountering the past and the present, coming across contemporary witnesses, traces, stories and pictures. I suggest to all those still waiting for a traditional interview that they visit the Motherhouse themselves. With a little imagination, everyone can dive into this world of prayer and charity. Being a fly on the wall of the Motherhouse will have you experiencing a typically Olpe kind of *"woman power"*!

"He Leads - I FOLLOW"

MISHAWAKA
07.10.1943

ROTTERDAM
25.11.1875

NEW-YORK
12.12.1875

OLPE

LAFAYETTE
14.12.1875

CHAPTER VII

"HE LEADS, WE FOLLOW" —
TO MISHAWAKA, INDIANA, USA:
FOUNDATION AND DEVELOPMENT OF
IMMACULATE HEART OF MARY EASTERN PROVINCE

Historical Development of the Province

On December 14, 1875, six German-speaking Sisters descended from the train and took the first steps upon their new home soil in Lafayette, Indiana. Their curious, yet determined gazes appeared from behind their black, *"stove-top pipe"*-shaped veils and their faces were set with a look of courageous resolve. Pulling their black woolen capes tightly around their rough brown habits cinctured with knotted cords, they picked up their small bags of belongings and shivered a bit as the winter winds blew through the train station. Thus began the history of the Sisters of St. Francis of Perpetual Adoration in the United States of America.

Sr. Clara Thomas, Sr. Bonaventura Heiliger, Sr. Agatha Schraer, Sr. Rose Schmidt, Sr. Augustina Dirkmann, and Sr. Alphonsa Neuhoff had spent the last month sailing the ocean and traveling across their new country in order to escape the religious persecution in their homeland caused by the difficulties placed upon the Sisters during the *"Kulturkampf"* (a time in which anti-Church sentiment and laws caused oppression for many Catholics, especially Religious Communities.) The work of the Sisters had been severely restricted, as well as their ability to receive new candidates into their Community. Just when the situation had become too overwhelming, their foundress, Mother Maria Theresia, was offered a ray of hope for her newly-founded Congregation in Olpe, Germany. She accepted the invitation of Bishop Joseph Dwenger to establish a convent within the city of Lafayette, located in the southeastern part of his diocese in Fort Wayne, Indiana.

Aline wants to know

What do you do all day long?

Every Sister has her task; she may work in the kitchen, the Host Bakery, the hospital, the nursing home or the office, depending on where she lives and what her profession is. We also have free time and go on vacation.

The Sisters' coming to Lafayette was unheralded and unsung. However, a few days later an article appeared in the local newspaper, which stated:

"The Sisters to the number of six who are to have charge of the new hospital in this city arrived on the train night before last. They are very intelligent and well-informed ladies and express themselves as greatly pleased with the country. They are going to work with a will to get their hospital in order, where they can properly care for the afflicted. They have secured a building, corner of Tenth and Cincinnati, and yesterday were out making purchases of articles needed immediately. And right here it may be stated that all donations of blankets, bedding, coal, wood, provisions, etc. will be thankfully received, and will be used to the best advantage."

At first, the Sisters settled in happily, occupying a small building which served as both hospital and convent, where they cared diligently for the sick and grew to know and love the people whom they served. Six months later, on June 11, 1876, the cornerstone of the first St. Elizabeth Hospital and Provincial House was laid. Despite the Sisters' insecurities and lack of the necessities of life, they had achieved their first objective – a Community in America.

Their little Community began to grow. Two years later, the Sisters were also able to begin their work in

education by taking charge of St. Boniface Elementary School in Lafayette. Once again, they were delighted to teach God's little ones as they had once done in their orphanage in Olpe, Germany.

The first years were replete with untold privations and hardships, but trust in God was equal to their great faith. The hourly rotation in perpetual adoration of our Lord in the Blessed Sacrament was the source of strength and courage to overcome all obstacles as they steadily grew in numbers and expansion. Within eleven years, 1876 -1887, the Community established six hospitals and assumed charge of seven schools

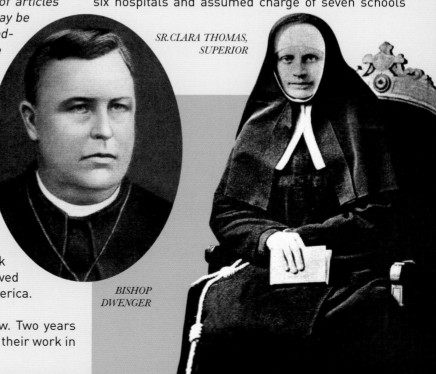

SR. CLARA THOMAS, SUPERIOR

BISHOP DWENGER

located in the states of Indiana, Ohio, Nebraska, and Kansas. Much to the delight of the pioneering Sisters, Mother Maria Theresia visited them in America to observe their progress on three separate occasions.

In 1886, because of the size of the Congregation and the larger number of houses in the United States and Germany, where the anti-clerical reaction had subsided, two Provinces were erected; the German Province with the Motherhouse in Olpe, Germany, and the American Province with its Provincialate in Lafayette, Indiana. Sr. Alphonsa Neuhoff, one of the pioneer Sisters, was appointed as the first Provincial Superior. Sisters from Germany continued to come to the United States each year until 1951, offering a sense of continuity to the growing Province.

THE SISTERS' HOUSE IN LAFAYETTE

ST. FRANCIS SCHOOL AND COLLEGE

VII

"HE LEADS, WE FOLLOW" – TO MISHAWAKA, INDIANA, USA:
FOUNDATION AND DEVELOPMENT OF IMMACULATE HEART OF MARY EASTERN PROVINCE

MOUNT ALVERNO IN MISHAWAKA, 1943

ST. BONIFACE SCHOOL IN LAFAYETTE
AROUND 1880

The progress of the Community in America was steady. Within a little more than fifty years, the field of labor had spread to such a wide area that the administration of the Community became increasingly difficult. At the request of Mother Verena, General Superior, application was made to Rome for the division of the American Province, which was granted in December, 1931.

It was divided into two Provinces: the Eastern, the Immaculate Heart of Mary Province, remained with the Lafayette Provincial House; and the Western, the St. Joseph Province, took up its headquarters at St. Anthony Hospital, Denver, Colorado until a suitable Provincial House could be erected.

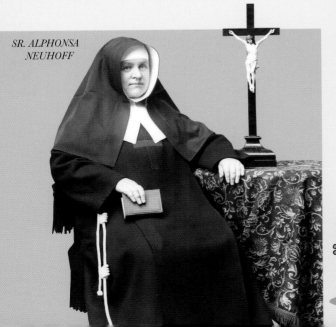

SR. ALPHONSA
NEUHOFF

As the number of Sisters in the Community, as well as the services provided at the Lafayette location grew, it became necessary to consider a different site for the Provincial House. At the urging of Bishop Noll, a home and surrounding land was purchased in Mishawaka, Indiana, and in 1943, the relocation of the Provincial House was made. Now referred to as "Mount Alverno," it became the site of the Provincial House and administration, the house of formation and the retirement home and infirmary for the Sisters. The same year also witnessed the move of St. Francis College (now the University of St. Francis) from the former provincial location to Fort Wayne, Indiana.

On the Lighter Side

On many Halloween evenings I would pass out treats to the kids who came to the door. One child said "I remember you wore that same costume last year!"

VII

"HE LEADS, WE FOLLOW" — TO MISHAWAKA, INDIANA, USA:
FOUNDATION AND DEVELOPMENT OF IMMACULATE HEART OF MARY EASTERN PROVINCE

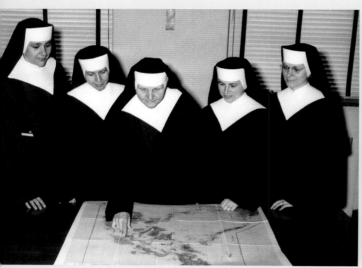

MISSIONARY WORK IN THE PHILIPPINES, 1962

In response to calls for assistance, four Sisters were sent to establish the first foreign mission in the Philippines in 1962. Due to their expansion and steady growth of new members, the Philippines became a Province in 1993. A similar mission activity occurred in Honduras, Central America, from 1978 to 1995, when the mission was turned over to the Franciscan Sisters of the Immaculate Conception, a native Congregation with its Provincial House in El Salvador.

The Province Today

The Province strives to follow the purpose and mission of the Congregation as expressed in the Mission Statement:

"We, the Sisters of St. Francis of Perpetual Adoration, participate in the mission of the Roman Catholic Church by living the Gospel after the example of St. Francis and our foundress, Mother Maria Theresia Bonzel. We strive to combine the contemplative life with the active through perpetual adoration and the works of mercy in education, healthcare, and other ecclesial ministries."

In their service to the Church, the Sisters follow Jesus who spent His public life in praying, teaching, healing, and ministering to others.

The Perpetual Adoration of our Lord in the Eucharist is carried out in the adoration chapel at the

PROVINCIALATE ON MOUNT ALVERNO IN MISHAWAKA

Provincial House by the Sisters in the main convent and adjoining retirement convent of Our Lady of the Angels.

A healthcare system which now has fourteen hospitals and other health-related clinics in both Indiana and Illinois, and a number of support services, has 18,200 employees, including approximately 600 physicians. In 2010, the healthcare system corporation's name was changed to Franciscan Alliance.

The ministry in higher education is continued at the University of St. Francis in Fort Wayne, Indiana, which currently enrolls over 1800 undergraduate students and almost 300 graduate students. The University's campus covers 108 acres and has some twenty buildings, including three residence halls.

The Sisters continue with their presence at St. Boniface School, Lafayette, Indiana, their first educational ministry in America. They also serve in some parish elementary schools, diocesan high schools, and other ecclesial ministries.

In addition to their apostolates, the Sisters are involved with other works of mercy, such as retreats,

CHAPEL OF PERPETUAL ADORATION

111

visiting the elderly in parishes and nursing homes, and serving in soup kitchens, homeless shelters, clinics for the poor, homes for unwed mothers, and "right-to-life" organizations.

As of January 1, 2011, the Province membership was 121, which included 104 perpetually professed Sisters, 8 temporary professed, 5 novices, and 4 postulants. The recent new members are a hopeful sign of growth in continuing the mission and dreams of Mother Maria Theresia. These Sisters also assist the Vocation Director in contacts with young women at various events and retreats at the Provincial House, as well as in schools, parishes, and dioceses.

Mount Alverno remains the *"hub"* of the Province. The Sisters are grateful to God to be nestled in this beautiful setting where the young Sisters can be formed in their religious life, where the senior Sisters can enjoy the more contemplative years of their life, where the primary apostolate of Perpetual Adoration can be carried out, and where all the Sisters of the Province can come *"home"* to celebrate Community gatherings and seek respite from the demands of their more active apostolates. It has also become a place they welcome their co-workers, visitors and groups with Franciscan hospitality. They share their facilities with bishops, the lay Third Order Franciscans as well as a vibrant Diocesan Youth Group. Priests, seminarians, adults, youth, parish and diocesan groups come to stay for retreats. With fewer Sisters visible in the hospitals and schools, it has been beneficial in hosting groups from these apostolates. It has been especially meaningful for them to visit the adoration chapel and know that the Sisters pray for them. In addition to this, many people come throughout the day to pray before the Blessed Sacrament.

As did the six pioneer Sisters who came to America over a century ago before them, the Sisters today adhere to the words of Mother Maria Theresia, who exhorted them, *"As we pray, so we live, and as our life, so our prayer."* The calling of the Sisters of St. Francis of Perpetual Adoration is to follow the Gospel of Jesus Christ after the example of St. Francis and Mother Maria Theresia Bonzel. They express their commitment through the vows of poverty, chastity, and obedience, in Community and in serving others. The Sisters believe that life in Community and service to others is fruitful only to the extent that it flows from prayer.

In gratitude to God for the gift of 150 years as a Congregation, the Sisters continue to live and cherish the motto of their foundress, Venerable Mother Maria Theresia Bonzel, *"He leads, I follow."*

CONVENT ON MOUNT ALVERNO IN MISHAWAKA

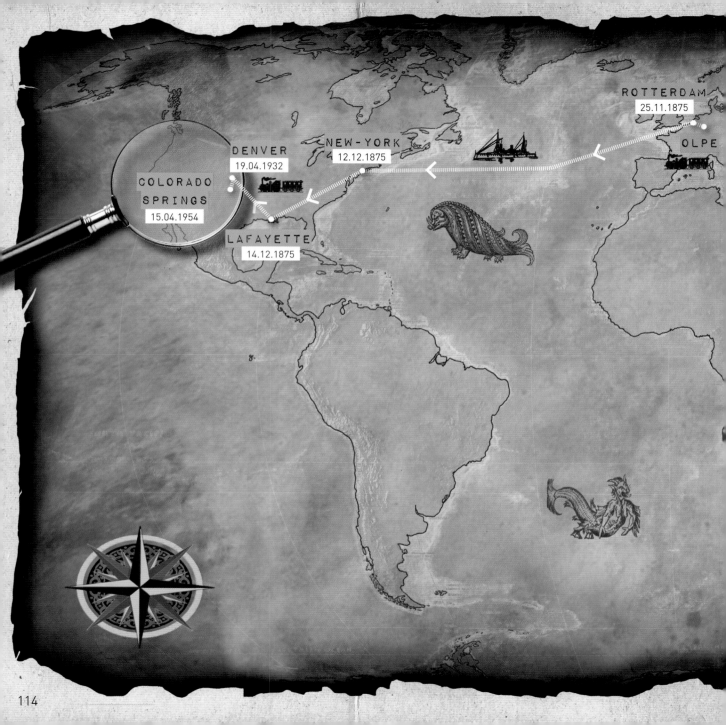

ROTTERDAM
25.11.1875

OLPE

DENVER
19.04.1932

NEW-YORK
12.12.1875

COLORADO
SPRINGS
15.04.1954

LAFAYETTE
14.12.1875

LOURDES GROTTO ON MOUNT ST. FRANCIS

CHAPTER **VIII**

"HE LEADS, I FOLLOW" - TO DENVER, COLORADO, USA: FOUNDATION AND DEVELOPMENT OF ST. JOSEPH WESTERN PROVINCE

During the late 1920's, a ruling in Canon Law decreed that a single American Province of the Sisters of Saint Francis of Perpetual Adoration, founded in Germany, was too large and too widespread to be properly administered by one Provincial Administration. Therefore, it was determined that the American Province would be divided into two Provinces: an Eastern Province, the Immaculate Heart of Mary Province, located in Lafayette, Indiana; and a Western Province, St. Joseph Province, located at St. Anthony Hospital in Denver, Colorado.

Plans for the separation into two Provinces began in 1930 when Mother Verena Schulte, the Superior General of the Congregation, visited the United States from Olpe, Germany. It was decided that Sister Bernarda Weller remain Provincial of the Eastern Province, and that Sister Basilia Kugler be appointed Provincial of the Western Province. The dedication of St. Joseph Province was held in the beautiful chapel of St. Anthony Hospital on March 19, the Feast of St. Joseph, in the year 1932.

During the period between 1875 and 1932, the American foundations spread over a vast area and comprised 12 states. The Sisters staffed 21 hospitals, 52 schools, and 4 orphanages. After the division into Provinces, the Western Province included the states of Colorado, Kansas, Nebraska, New Mexico, and Wyoming (10 hospitals; 26 schools; one college; 3 orphanages). The beginnings of the Province were difficult. The culture of the western area of the United States differed vastly from the culture of the eastern area of the United States. Geographically, the West consisted of wide-open spaces with many miles separating cities and states, which in the early years,

ST. ANTHONY HOSPITAL IN DENVER, COLORADO, 1932

119

made travelling difficult. In many areas, the climate was arid and not conducive to farming. The social and religious backgrounds of the people in the West also differed from those in the East. For many years, the Sisters served the very poor in Hispanic communities and Native American pueblos and reservations in New Mexico and Kansas. Therefore, their financial resources were meager, and the Sisters worked hard to meet their own basic human needs and those of the people they served.

Nevertheless, with its humble beginnings, and under the leadership of Mother Basilia, the young Province began to develop. Although the novitiate remained in Lafayette, on June 29, 1933, the first profession of vows ceremony was held in Saint Joseph Province, at which time 5 Sisters pronounced their perpetual vows.

On May 24, 1941, permission was granted from the Sacred Congregation in Rome to establish a novitiate in the St. Joseph Province in Denver. On August 15, 13 novices, who had entered from the West, went to Denver from Lafayette to continue their novitiate. Also, at this time 6 postulants entered the Congregation in Denver. The establishment of the novitiate in Denver gave the newly-founded Province a firm foundation.

The next big step was to authorize permanent membership in the Provinces. No steps had been taken since its founding in 1932 to determine which Sisters belonged to which Province. The date set for each Sister to cast her ballot to indicate which Province she chose to belong, was February 11, 1942. The number of Sisters who chose to belong to the Western Province was 412; that of the Eastern Province was 448. The first reception in St. Joseph Province was

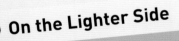

On the Lighter Side

Besides being a full time teacher, I was also a full time sacristan in many parishes. One morning before Mass I had just stepped out of the room for a minute. One of the priests came to my classroom. When I returned one child said, "Sister, a priest was looking for you." I asked "Which one?" and he answered promptly, "The one who grows hair only on the edges is all I know."

SR. BASILIA KUGLER 1. PROVINCIAL SUPERIOR

held on August 12, 1942: 9 postulants received the habit; 6 Sisters pronounced temporary profession of vows; and 5 Sisters pronounced perpetual vows. Thus, as of August 12, 1942, the total number of professed members in St. Joseph Province was 418.

Home, a home previously used for the elderly and operated by the Episcopal Church in Denver, the Sisters decided that the property and buildings were excellent for a new Provincialate, and they made the purchase on May 12, 1943. The Provincial offices and

JEMEZ PUEBLO DANCER IN NEW MEXICO

The suite of rooms at St. Anthony Hospital was no longer adequate to accommodate the needs of St. Joseph Province, and a search began for an alternative location. After careful inspection of the Oakes

novitiate were moved from St. Anthony Hospital to the Oakes Home during the latter part of August and the dedication of St. Joseph Convent, as it was named, occurred on December 14, 1943. Shortly after settling in the new location, the School of the Aspirants was opened in August 1944 and accredited through Cathedral High School in Denver. It was the hope that the Aspirancy would be an opening for new membership into the Province.

Another important blessing and date in the history of St. Joseph Province was April 28, 1952. Mother Fabiana Schulte, the Mother General, along with Mother Reginalda Gerlach, Provincial, and her Council, met with Mr. Blevins Davis, owner of the Modern Woodmen of America Sanatorium with its 1,400 acres of land, and also the owner of an elegant estate known as the Trianon, both in Colorado Springs. Mr. Davis had inherited a fortune from his wife, Marguerite Davis, who had inherited millions from her first husband, James B. Hill, a pioneer American railroad magnate. Mrs. Davis died in 1948, leaving over two million dollars exclusively for charity. Mr. Davis offered to give the Marguerite Davis charitable fund to the Sisters of St. Francis if they would purchase the Woodmen Estate and the Trianon. The Sisters gratefully received the Davis charitable fund and subsequently purchased the Woodmen Estate and the Trianon. The deeds to the newly acquired property were transferred to St. Joseph Province in January, 1953. The Provincialate was moved from Denver to the Woodmen property in Colorado Springs in the spring of 1954, and after the dedication on March 15, 1954, the newly acquired gift soon took on the name of St. Joseph Province at Mount Saint Francis. The Trianon, because of its elegance, did not lend itself well to the

OAKES HOME, WHICH BECAME THE DENVER PROVINCIALATE IN 1943

mission of the Sisters. Therefore, the Sisters were grateful when the property was sold in August, 1960. With the proceeds of the sale, the Sisters were able to build a new beautiful, circular Chapel which was dedicated on April 23, 1963.

The years of the 1960's through the 70's were rather unsettling years for religious life throughout the United States, and St. Joseph Province was no exception. Many internal changes occurred due to adaptations promoted by the Documents of Vatican II. It was during this period that many Sisters received dispensations from their vows and left the Congregation. It was also during this period that many Sisters felt called to serve in positions other than the traditional practices of healthcare and education and elected to minister primarily in parishes, pastoral care in hospitals, and in areas of social services.

WOODMEN SANATORIUM AROUND 1900

Aline wants to know

Does your room have a TV?

No, we all share one television.

TRIANON IN COLORADO SPRINGS, 1954

SR. STEPHANIE MCREYNOLDS

SR. ROSE MARIE IMIG

WILL IAM P. RYAN, JR

HERMAN H. GUENTHER

Therefore, with the diminishment in members and Sisters choosing other areas of ministry, the Province had to make alternative plans with its hospitals and schools. One of the first initiatives was to band all their healthcare institutions to form The Franciscan Healthcare Corporation, finalized in 1981, for the purposes of containing costs and preserving their mission and values. Eventually, this led to the consolidation of The Franciscan Healthcare Corporation with the health system of the Sisters of Charity of Cincinnati, Ohio, and later, to the relinquishment of their sponsorship in 1995. Also, during this period (1970's and 80's), the Sisters gradually withdrew from many of their long-established schools, including their college, the University of Albuquerque, previously known as The College of St. Joseph.

The decrease in new members, the increase of older members and the transition away from traditional ministries had an impact on Mount Saint Francis. With fewer financial resources to meet the retirement needs of the Sisters, the Province began to look at options to best use their resources. A major decision was made in the late 1970's to sell a major portion of Mount St. Francis property, and on July 10, 1978, the Colorado Springs City Council approved the Peregrine Development Project. Along with the sale of many acres of the property, studies were conducted

ST. JOSEPH COLLEGE/ UNIVERSITY
IN ALBUQUERQUE

on the best use of Mount St. Francis property and buildings, and a major renovation occurred in the mid 1980's, which established three viable ministries: 1) a Skilled Care Nursing Center; 2) a Retreat Center; and 3) a Counseling Center. During this time, a retirement trust fund was also established to care for the future needs of the Sisters.

In the 1990's a second renovation occurred on the campus. The construction of Canticle Chapel provided a beautiful and inspiring place where the Sisters gathered daily, and continue to gather, to celebrate the Eucharistic Liturgy, pray their Hours of Adoration, pray the Divine Office, and spend time in personal reflection and contemplation. At this time, additional living spaces for the Sisters were created, and a building was renovated to accommodate more conference and meeting rooms for the Retreat Center.

Another paradigm shift occurred in 2002 when the Provincial Council determined that the Sisters needed professional expertise in finance and management to secure the viability of their Mount Saint Francis ministries. The first lay Chief Executive Officer, Mason Smith, was hired in 2002, and the ministries became stable through many necessary changes and adaptations.

Today, the reality is that the Sisters are few in number (58) with an average age of 77, but they still maintain the tenacity and determination to keep their Mission alive and their Franciscan charism afire. They have grown in their awareness that Evangelical Life is not established around a common place or

MEETING OF ALL SISTERS ON MOUNT ST. FRANCIS

around a common task. It is rather formed around their Franciscan Mission and Vision—to live the Gospel simply and to minister to the poor in their midst. It is this understanding of Evangelical Life that has guided their Province into diverse ministries and diverse life styles, while never compromising their vowed life or their commitment to Adoration, Eucharist, Contemplation/Prayer, Community and Service.

The Provincialate, Mount Saint Francis, is the core of the Sisters' lives — it is their home and the center of their spiritual lives — Perpetual Adoration; it is their Administration Headquarters; it is their Formation Center; it is the Justice, Peace and Integrity of Creation Center; it is the Center of the Companion Relationship Program, which is a way of inviting lay people to journey with the Sisters in their search for a deeper Franciscan spirituality. Mount Saint Francis is also the core of their service to the Church as they partner with lay men and women in leadership and skilled positions. They continue to maintain three viable ministries at the Mount: 1) a 108 bed skilled-care Nursing Center for the frail elderly, both lay and religious; 2) a Retreat Center which serves over 10,000 people annually; and 3) a Counseling Center which ministers to almost 100 clients monthly. The Sisters' ministries employ around 240 persons, many of whom are at the lower economic level. In addition, the Sisters leased their circular chapel and one adjacent building to the Diocese of Colorado Springs so that a parish could be established on campus. They also leased a building for an Autism Center for children.

In the city of Colorado Springs, they founded Women Partnering, a ministry that serves financially vulnerable women and children, especially unwanted and unappreciated immigrants.

Beyond the Provincialate, some Sisters serve in healthcare institutions as nurses or pastoral minis-

ters, in parish ministry, and in other areas of volunteer works in the states of California, Colorado, Nebraska and New Mexico.

As a Province, the Sisters face their challenges with hope. As they continue to embrace the reality of their diminishment, they also embrace the reality that even though they are fewer in numbers, they are not less in spirit. Their Mission and Charism continue to be kept alive by the dedication and commitment of Sisters and laity working together. They have laid the groundwork

Mother Maria Theresia Bonzel: *"All is in God's hands; and when we do what we can, we can be calm."*

for their service to continue into the future. They are grateful for the bountiful gifts God has bestowed on them as a Congregation and as a Province. They are reminded of the words of their beloved Foundress,

MISHAWAKA
09.09.1962

SAN FRANCISCO
13.09.1962

MANILA
04.10.1962

BAYBAY
11.10.1962

A RICE FIELD

CHAPTER IX

"HE LEADS, WE FOLLOW" -
TO THE PHILIPPINES:
PROVINCE OF THE IMMACULATE CONCEPTION

When the Immaculate Heart of Mary Province in Mishawaka, Indiana, chose to open their first foreign mission in the Philippines, they fulfilled one of Mother Maria Theresia's special dreams nearly a century after the foundation of the Congregation in 1863. In January, 1962, Mother M. Philotera Meirose and her Council agreed to open a mission, Immaculate Conception Province, in Baybay, Leyte, after considering the request of the Franciscan Fathers already working in the Philippines. Many Sisters responded to the request for volunteers. From them Mother and the Council selected Sr. Denise Stolinski, Superior, Sr. Annette Crone, Sr. Mary Paul Pfautsch, and Sr. Mark Orgon.

The realization of this historic event began with the Departure Ceremony for the four pioneers on September 8, 1962. Accompanied by Mother Philotera and Sr. Josetta Schoenle, the small group traveled by bus to Chicago on September 9, and continued the journey by train to San Francisco, where they finally boarded the SS President Cleveland on September 13 for the 21-day trip to Manila. The Franciscan Fathers

from Baybay met them at the port and helped them get their cargo through Customs; some FMM Sisters (Franciscans Missionary of Mary) assisted them in getting through the necessary Immigration Offices. After a flight from Manila to Cebu, they were ready to experience their first inter-island boat ride to Baybay, where the faculty and students of *"Franciscan College of the Immaculate Conception"* (FCIC) welcomed

THE SISTERS' FIRST CONVENT BUILDING, 1962

131

them to their new home on October 11. The FCIC Band enthusiastically greeted them with the song, *"Oh, You Beautiful Doll"*.

Their first convent, a very old Spanish-style structure, was located right along the seashore. This served as their residence for the next four years. Being so far away from *"home,"* the Sisters anxiously looked forward to their first Provincial Visitation on August 30, 1963, when Mother Philotera and Sr. Josetta arrived. Among the important things to be discussed during this first visit was the possible location of a new convent. Already young ladies were beginning to express an interest in entering the Community, and the possibility of candidates joining them would necessitate more space. With the help of the Fathers, Mother Philotera and the Sisters selected a site — *"a hill"* — that would hopefully meet their future needs. Construction was begun on February 7, 1965. In October of this same year, while still living by the sea, Mother Francesco Bruggemann arrived for the first General Visitation.

The first Filipina Postulant, Miss Cecilia Caintic, was accepted on February 2, 1965. She was invested with the habit on September 8 and became known as Sr. Francis. Several years later, Sister requested to transfer to a Poor Clare Monastery, where she continues to live as a contemplative nun until the present time. God continued to bless the new Philippine mission with vocations, so that it soon showed promising signs of growth. When the Sisters moved from their initial seaside residence to the new convent being constructed on the nearby hill on February 7, 1966, there were already four novices and seven postulants with the American Sisters.

Aline wants to know

Do you have a game console?

No. I don't need one.

Sr. Andrew Beckman arrived from the States on October 22, 1966, to help with the growing Community. When Sr. Annette returned to the States after 5 ½ years of missionary service, she was replaced by Sr. Joseph Ann Vogel on July 23, 1969. In 1974, Sr. Mark returned home after 11 ½ years of missionary work. Sr. Andrew also returned to the States in 1974, having helped the Community there for 7 ½ years. Sr. Dianne Zimmer arrived in the Philippines on Oct. 6, 1974, and worked in FCIC until she returned to the States 18 months later.

Early Growth and Expansion

With the growth of the Community, it became possible to accept the first mission: Sto. Niño Academy in Malitbog, Southern Leyte. For many years it had been under the administration of a private lay corporation. They were interested in donating it to us, confident that we would maintain its Catholic identity. The Sisters assumed the ownership and administration of the Academy in June, 1970. Shortly after this, the Franciscan Fathers expressed their desire to discontinue their work in education at FCIC and concentrate on pastoral work. On January 1, 1971, the Sisters officially assumed the ownership and administration of FCIC with Sr. Mary Paul serving as the first Sister Directress. When the government implemented Filipinization of administrative positions in the schools in 1976, Sr. Grace Gerong became the

first Filipina Directress. Although the Sisters now work in many other schools, these first two educational centers are the only ones under the ownership of the Community.

New missions were opened where the Sisters continued their apostolates of Education, Catechetics, Campus Ministry, and Retreat work. At present, these include the following: Cebu City, Cebu — 1975; Maasin, So. Leyte — 1979; Tacloban City, Leyte — 1979; Carigara, Leyte — 1984; St. Bernard, So. Leyte

135

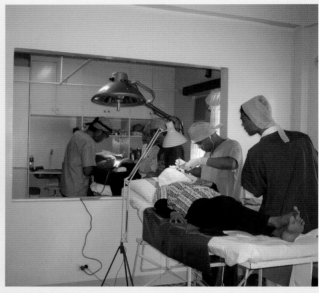

BONZEL-HEALTH-CENTER IN BAYBAY

— 1987; Dagami, Leyte — 1992; Tagbilaran City, Bohol — 1996; Isabel, Leyte — 1999, and Maghaway, Talisay, Cebu - 1999. The centers where the Sisters work are either privately owned or are under the jurisdiction of a diocese.

An outstanding event in the memory of many Sisters was the tragic Super-typhoon Asiang (January 8, 1972) that made a direct path across the town of Baybay and left extensive damage in its path. As the storm raged through the area, its winds reached 185 kilometers per hour, but traveled at the speed of only 11 kilometers per hour, thus remaining for a long time in one place. As people fled the flood waters overtaking the town, they sought higher ground at FCIC and Sacred Heart Convent. There were approximately 2000 who occupied the classrooms at FCIC; when that was filled, another 1000 gathered at the convent where they stayed for the next 20 hours. Those who sought safety at the convent had brought no food provisions. Using what the Sisters had on hand, they provided two nourishing servings of stew, one in the late morning and another in the late afternoon. By 4:00 a.m. the next morning, people ventured back to their homes only to discover 18 inches of mud. The clean-up and the repairs continued for many months thereafter. The electricity was not restored to the town for the next six months; everyone in the town carried every drop of water in buckets for the next two years.

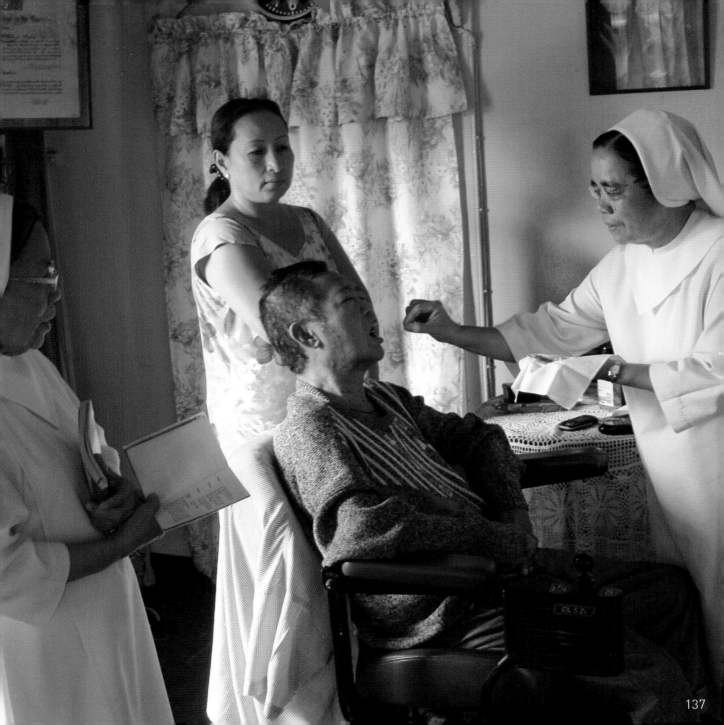

IX "HE LEADS, WE FOLLOW" - TO THE PHILIPPINES: PROVINCE OF THE IMMACULATE CONCEPTION

On May 1, 1976, the Immaculate Conception Region was established. Appointed by Mishawaka to lead the new Region were Sr. Mary Paul, Regional Superior, Sr. Joseph Ann, Regional Vicar, and Sr. Denise, Sr. Christine Suarez, and Sr. Anthony Kuizon, Regional Councilors.

By October 4, 1975, there were a sufficient number of Sisters at Sacred Heart Convent to begin keeping adoration through the night hours — from 9:00 p.m. to 5:00 a.m. in the Main Chapel without the Blessed Sacrament exposed. Since there are no screens on the Chapel windows, it was a real challenge to control the mosquitoes that are usually plentiful in the dark. Nearly two years later on Ash Wednesday, February 23, 1977, Perpetual Adoration was begun in the Main Chapel. However, the Blessed Sacrament was still not exposed since there was not sufficient space to open a special Chapel for that purpose. The feast of the Immaculate Conception, December 8, 1978, marked the opening of the newly-prepared Perpetual Adoration Chapel with the Blessed Sacrament exposed. The Sisters were joyful that at least we could feel we were now fully participating in our primary apostolate — Perpetual Adoration.

The first straw mats Chapter was celebrated in January, 1987. What a marvelous event it was with all the Sisters gathered for the weekend, combining the spiritual, the inspirational, and the social! It was unanimously agreed that this gathering would be held every two years, if possible.

The Community in the Philippines celebrated its Silver Jubilee on October 3, 1987. Since many priests, Sisters, faculty and staff members, benefactors,

On the Lighter Side

Children observe what priests wear also. Normally, the Pastor would come to the school dressed in his clerical suit. One day a first grader said to me, "Hey, Sister, I know this is report card day. Father is wearing his report card clothes. I saw him coming across the playground!" (Father was wearing his cassock). So, when he came into our classroom to distribute the cards, he told the kids they were a great bunch and they all would be happy to see their grades. He said, "A is for Awful; B is for Better; C is for Careful; D is for Dandy!" One kid spoke out: "That's not right — D is for Dumb!"

138

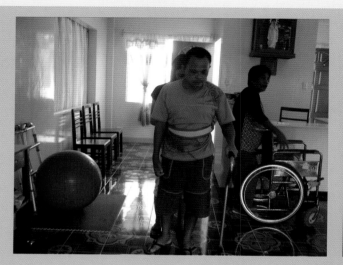

BONZEL-HEALTH-CENTER / PHYSIOTHERAPY IN BAYBAY

and friends would be in attendance, it was arranged to celebrate the Jubilee Mass in the Parish Church. Following the Holy Mass, a dinner was catered in the FCIC Gym.

With the increase in the Community's membership, Sacred Heart Convent was becoming very overcrowded, especially when the Sisters wanted to be together for special occasions: Investiture, Profession, Retreat, Community Days, etc. Permission was given to erect a separate building for the novitiate. Groundbreaking for this took place on October 6, 1987. By February 21, 1989, the novices and postulants were able to move into the new building — St. Martin de Porres Novitiate. With much more space now available in Sacred Heart

Convent, it was possible to rearrange and provide better space for the Regional Offices, as well as other departments.

Amidst the joys of the growing Community was the death of the first Filipina Sister, Sr. Clare Peñon, on July 6, 1988. Her loss was deeply felt by everyone, since we had all been so very close for many years. The years 2002, 2005, and 2009 were marked with the death of three more Sisters. These are all buried in the Sisters' Cemetery on our property in the Philippines.

A landmark in our history that touched all the Provinces was the establishment of the Philippines as the Immaculate Conception Province on January

1, 1993. Gathered for the occasion were Sr. Xaveria Kronen, Superior General from Olpe; Sr. Eremburga Schafer, Provincial Superior from the North Province in Werl, Germany; Sr. Bonifacis Edenfeld, Provincial Superior from the South Province in Bonn, Germany; Sr. Philothea Kahl, General Secretary from Olpe, who served as the official translator; Sr. Rose Agnes Pfautsch, Provincial Superior from the Eastern Province in Mishawaka; and Sr. Clarice Gentrup, Provincial Superior from the Western Province in Colorado Springs. The official proclamation was held on January 10, allowing travel time after the Christmas holidays for all the guests to arrive, avoiding the heavy flight schedules immediately surrounding the New Year. Sr. Mary Paul was appointed the first Provincial Superior, Sr. Joseph Ann, Provincial Vicar, and Provincial Councilors: Sr. Anthony Kuizon, Sr. Veronica Tulipas, Sr. Emilie Igano, Sr. Myra Seratubias, and Sr. Teresita Lopez.

Since this was the first time in the history of the Congregation that there were five Provinces, Sr. Xaveria took the opportunity to hold an *"International Meeting"* with the Provincials — the first of its kind. The Philippines was honored to host this historic gathering in January, 1993.

In addition to Sacred Heart Convent and the Novitiate Building, a Grotto in honor of the Blessed Mother was erected on the property between the two buildings on December 10, 1994. Since that time, weather permitting, the Sisters form a procession from the Main Chapel to the Grotto every Saturday evening before the recitation of Evening Office.

A small piece of property along the seashore in Bunga, Leyte, about 13 kilometers from Baybay, was purchased in 1996 for the purpose of providing a Rest House for the Sisters to enjoy a relaxing atmosphere away from the public eye. The site was named *"Marymont"* and consists of an outdoor picnic area and a small house where the Sisters can rest, after enjoying a swim in the cool waters of the sea. The first picnic was held there on September 8, 1996, the Sisters name's day.

During the General Chapter in Germany in July, 1997, the structure of the General Leadership was revised and Council members were chosen to represent each Province. Representing the Philippine Province on the General level for the first time was Sr. Grace Gerong, who served a six-year term.

At the Provincial Chapter in July, 1998, it was decided that the Community in the Philippines needed to begin considering the turnover of the Province from American leadership to Filipino leadership. To initiate this process, Sr. Phyllis Bulawan was elected the first Filipino Provincial. Sr. Joseph Ann was asked to continue one additional term as the Vicar; the Council consisted of Sr. Mary Paul and four Filipino Sisters.

The first OSF International Vocation and Formation meeting was held from February 7-13, 1999. In attendance were Sr. Rose Marie Imig and Sr. Frances Sedlacek from Colorado Springs; Sr. Angela Mellady, Sr. Lois DeLee, and Sr. Jacinta Krecek from Mishawaka; Sr. Sigrid Brieden, Sr. Magdalena Krol, and Sr. Grace Gerong from Germany; and Sr. Judith Lorica, Sr. Veronica Tulipas, Sr. JoEllen Ramirez, and Sr. Myra Seratubias from the Philippines.

A joyous *"reunion"* took place in March, 2000, when Sr. Andrew and Sr. Dianne were able to make a trip back to Baybay to experience first-hand the progress and the changes that had taken place since their earlier assignments here in 1966 and 1974, nearly 25 years earlier. The days of their visit passed all too quickly, but they were able to visit almost all of the missions where the Sisters were now working and were very pleased to see the progress that had been made.

The Philippine Province hosted its first International Gathering from April 20-30, 2007, when Sr. Mediatrix Nies invited 22 representatives of the *"young"* Sisters from each Province and the Brazil mission for a joint meeting, primarily for the purpose of Community bonding. Coming from Germany were Sr. Petra Brinkschulte, a member of the General Council who served as translator, Sr. Franziska Passeck, Sr. Gertrudis Luneborg, Sr. Marion Elfriede, and Sr. Josefa Teschner. Representing the Brazil mission were Sr. Neves Policarpo and Sr. Itelvanira Gomez. The delegates from Colorado Springs were Sr. Regina Marie Massarotti, Sr. Frances Sedlacek, Sr. Nadine Heimann, and Sr. Jeannette Kneifel. The Mishawaka delegates included Sr. Rose Hasser, Sr. Clare Reuille, Sr. Cheryl Dazey, and Sr. Ruth Luthman. Our Province was represented by Sr. Rosario Aya-ay, Sr. Lucretia Lebajan, Sr. Ida Porol, Sr. Annette Escasinas, Sr. Judith Lorica, Sr. Adrianne Siano, Sr. Louella Mangmang, and Sr. Consuelo Abian. The 10 days were filled with spiritual, cultural, and social activities, as well as fruitful discussions.

When it became necessary to provide additional space at the Provincialate, the construction of an extension to the main convent was completed early in 2011. All the Sisters are deeply grateful for all forms of support given by the Sisters in Germany, in Mishawaka, and in Colorado Springs. You have all been responsible for making the Philippine Province a reality.

HAMBURG
29.08.1963

OLPE

SÃO LUÍS
09.10.1963

FORTALEZA
20.09.1963

A COLORFUL LOOK AT LIFE

CHAPTER X "HE LEADS, WE FOLLOW" — THE "SONHO DE ALINE" (DREAM OF ALINE) PROJECT IN NORTHEASTERN BRAZIL

We chose the name for our children's project in memory of our foundress's birth name. Looking after children was one of the very first things she did. *"Aline"* is any girl in need of a feeling of security which we can give her.

"Prevention and Care: Let Me Hope and Dream" — this is our motto. It describes our preventative work and personal care for children and adolescents.

Dream of Aline was founded in Saõ José de Ribamar in Maranhaõ, northeastern Brazil, by the Sisters of the Brazilian convents of the

Sisters of St. Francis of Perpetual Adoration. Our aim is to support the development of vulnerable children from extremely poor families through various activities, workshops, and family visits. At this time we have 315 children. We make sure that the children have the opportunity to grow up in good physical, mental, spiritual and social conditions based on human dignity, freedom and every person's right to life as expressed in the Brazilian *"Law on the Protection of Children and Adolescents"*.

On the Lighter Side

The word "brown" brings to my mind other episodes- years ago. Little Mike asked, "Is that all you see in your cupbord is brown?" I answered,Yes, but they are all different." He could not believe they were the same, so I added: the one I wear on Saturday is different. Immediately he asked,"What color is that one?"

Many days I would wear a dressy suit to school; and other days I would choose to wear a vest, long -sleeved blouse, and skirt. The kindergarten room was directly across from first grade. I was standing in the doorway when a kindergartener came across the hallway. She stepped over to me and said, "Sister, you look so cute in that outfit today!" I thanked her and said, I'm so happy to hear that; I'll wear the same thing tomorrow."

What this means for our work:

To listen, show respect, and facilitate tenderness is what we expect from everyone working with our children and adolescents, because this is what is missing in the families and schools, in the favelas and neighborhoods.

The project offers the following activities: computer studies, handiwork, embroidery, self-defense, sports, ballet, guitar, flute and folk-dance classes, as well as homework help and other leisure activities. We also offer psychological care, a thematic approach to the integrity of creation, spirituality, and help with other everyday issues such as sexual violence, drug-abuse, personal hygiene and the rights and duties of every person.

Among the many activities during the year we put special emphasis on civic and religious holidays, e.g. Week of Culture, Mother's Day, Week of the Oneness of Creation, Christmas, Campaign for Fraternity, Lent, Holy Week, Easter, and others. Everyone loves participating in these festivities. Our staff, children, adolescents and Sisters treat each other well and with respect, which helps everyone to integrate.

Sister Maria José and Sister Francisca
Project Managers, April 2011

X "HE LEADS, WE FOLLOW" — THE "SONHO DE ALINE" (DREAM OF ALINE) PROJECT IN NORTHEASTERN BRAZIL

In this letter we, the children and adolescents of the *"Dream of Aline"* project, would like to express our pride and our gratitude for your help. Our thanks go to the Sisters and all sponsors. *"Dream of Aline"* is a place full of affection, understanding and friendship.

Here we are given the opportunity to dream of a better world. Children from difficult family backgrounds come here to receive a better foundation for their future. Adolescents who don't see a perspective for themselves find a family that listens and understands. All of us in the project form one big family whose members treat each other with respect.

My name is Andrelina Vilar. I am 17 years old and attend the project in the mornings. Today my outlook on life is very different; thanks to the project.

We gain a lot of new experiences together. I have learned to laugh and dance again, met many kind people and made new friends. I am thankful to everyone who has made it possible for us to already live our dreams a little. This has only happened because of people's solidarity with us.

My name is Nathaline and I joined the project when I was 12 years old. I am 15 now and go there every day after school. We are so happy that you look after us. We, the children and adolescents, want to tell you how important this project is for us.

Through participating in the many activities and events we are helped to develop our own personalities and receive a lot of love from the Sisters working for and with us. The project offers many workshops: computer studies, handiwork, homework, ballet, self-defense and much more.

We thank the Sisters and all the sponsors for their help. Their solidarity with us allows us to develop in different ways than before, and to learn a lot.

May God guard you and your paths.

Thank you for everything.

151

"He leads - I follow"

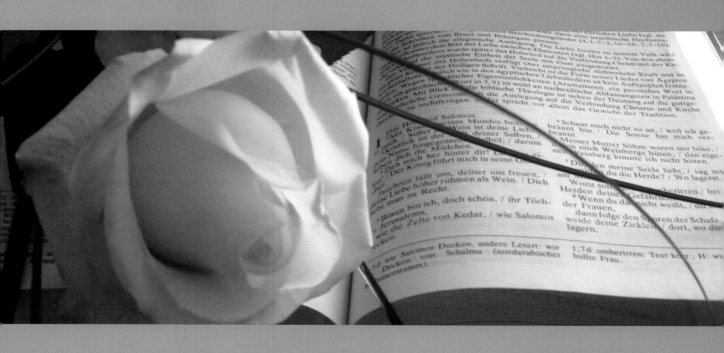

Chapter **XI** "To Adore and to Work" —
on the Community's Spirituality

Heribert Arens OFM

"Following the example of our holy father Francis, the Sisters strive to combine the contemplative with the active life in perpetual adoration and in acts of mercy." These are the words found in the General Constitution of the Sisters of St. Francis of Perpetual Adoration of Olpe. In a letter to me the General Superior, Sr. Magdalena, hit the nail on the head: *"to adore and to work."*

These two words remind me of a document that the UISG (International Union of Superiors General) published in 2004 entitled *"Passion for Christ, Passion for Humanity."* In the middle of this document are two biblical icons: the picture of the Woman at the Well and that of the Good Samaritan. Both are named and used as role models for an active life in a religious order.

The Samaritan Recognizes Need

Most of us are familiar with the Samaritan: he spots the victim of a robbery on the roadside, recognizes the challenge and acts quickly and decisively. The Sisters' and Brothers' charitable work is often interpreted in this way, and rightly so. The way the Samaritan acts is a model for our own actions. It starts with looking, not looking away. I have to recognize need. How else would I help? How much need do I pass every day that does not make me act because I simply do not see it? I am often so preoccupied with myself that with my head full of thoughts, or devoid of them, I even walk past good friends without noticing them. Thus I may not even say hello to them, let alone help in a situation of need. Either that or I am full of prejudices - I may be thinking *"He is just lazy!" "They should try and help themselves!" "This is none of my business — after all,*

we have lots of charities that can help!" I can see but do not see! The Samaritan saw! He saw not only with his eyes, but also with his heart. And this is when he recognized the injured man's dire situation and acted.

Courage and Kindness

He helped with courage and kindness where he was needed, not only with his heart but also with reason. Where the heart is the sole ruler, a lack of judgment prevails, which makes me suffocate the other with my love: *"But I only mean well!"* The Samaritan has heart but also reason; he thinks and considers. He thinks ahead — the man will need care and company in the future, too, and that is what he ensures.

To see with your eyes and your heart, to be open for contact with others, to help with kindness and courage: these are the Samaritan's motives he might not even be aware of. It is a model for everyone who acts in the here and now.

"He often withdrew to lonely places and prayed." (Luke 5:16)

But this is not everything. Jesus showed us in his own life that there is something else. Luke the Evangelist, in particular, depicts Jesus as someone who cared for those in need just like the Samaritan did. To this one dimension of Jesus' life, Luke adds a second one: he repeatedly mentions that Jesus withdrew for prayer, to be close to the Father and to gain renewed strength for His service to humanity. He did this so consistently that He also withdrew from the people asking for Him. Jesus knew that life had to be directed towards God, that it had to be anchored within Him, as otherwise all actions would become empty. In other words: being there only for others, wearing oneself out and expending all of one's strength on other people weakens the individual; it drains him of energy. In the end it would serve no-one. A river that only flows without being replenished and strengthened by rain or its tributaries silts up and dries out. If the only thing you do is give, your reserves will soon be depleted.

The Woman at the Well

That is why the Woman at the Well is connected with the Good Samaritan. She draws water from the well and fills her jugs. Yet she also draws from another well; Jesus who sits beside her. She feels His presence and knows that He has the water that can really quench her thirst and longing.

She has often pondered this longing in her life. That is why she starts to ask questions. At first they are quite superficial, but become much more existential. She wants to discover the Well's - Jesus'- secret. The conversation ends with the notion that Jesus *"may be the Messiah"* — the well starts to gush.

Action through Faith

Our actions need this encounter with Jesus as their foundation. Without this foundation, our actions become aimless acting for the sake of acting; we would get lost in blind activity. Without this foundation our actions can easily turn into ostentation with the aim of demonstrating how good and charitable we are, how selfless, what a blessing for humanity. Luke recounts in his Gospel that Jesus healed ten lepers; but only one returns to Him. Jesus was then moved to ask: *"Were not all ten cleansed? Where are the other nine? Was no one found to return and give praise to God except this foreigner?"* (Luke 17, 17:18). Here we need to listen carefully. He does not say: *"... to thank me"* but *"... to give praise to God."* It is not the aim of action through faith to draw attention to oneself and one's actions. In fact, the good I do is meant to point to Him who is the giver of all good. Action through faith is the annunciation of the healing God.

Contemplation

It requires people who do not get lost in blind activity but who remain at the well from which they drink and let others drink through their actions. It requires people who develop a sensitivity for looking beneath the surface to recognize the giver of all gifts behind the gifts we receive, to see the origin of all beauty behind the beautiful, and behind all suffering — the compassionate God. In other words: it requires people who maintain a contemplative lifestyle in all their actions, who are not satisfied by appearance but strive to look beyond the surface of things and thus to get ever closer to their secret.

Adoration

This is where adoration starts.

What do I adore during adoration? A piece of bread? What is so adorable about that? Francis guides us towards the secret: *"Let the entire man be seized with fear; let the whole world tremble; let heaven exult when Christ, the Son of the Living God, is on the altar in the hands of the priest. O admirable height and stupendous condescension! O humble sublimity! O sublime humility! That the Lord of the universe, God and the Son of God, so humbles Himself that for our salvation He hides Himself under a morsel of bread. Consider, brothers, the humility of God and pour out your hearts before Him, and be ye humbled that ye may be exalted by Him."* (Letter to All the Friars.) This contemplative lifestyle has the ability to recognize the Lord in a humble piece of bread. He who recognizes or even just senses the Lord is ready for adoration.

Such adoration helps to put things into perspective. There are too many people who turn themselves into God and bow not before the tabernacle but before their own reflection. There are too many who pray to their *"gods:"* influential politicians, wealthy bankers, soccer players, stars and starlets, their cars, their free time and freedom. Many a *"god"* in our society finds his *"adorer."* Yet may no one believe that this makes our world more humane. Even we Religious Congregations quickly develop a sense of pride when the mayor, the head of the district, or the senator announces a visit. It is easy to forget the "normal" people, those without status and with much simpler lives.

Even so-called celebrities are merely God's creatures, who together with me bow down before the Lord (the majority of them know this and do not want to be treated differently). He who bows before the true God contributes to more humanity in this world, in which everyone knows that God alone is our Lord. No other gods stand beside Him. I adore Him alone.

Adoration:
The foundation of a more humane world

This is how the humble act of adoration becomes a significant contribution to a more humane world:

If I know that God is the Lord, I do not have to be reminded that the person by my side is His creature as well, and that we walk through life *"arm in arm"* (W. Willms) instead of elbowing and fighting each other.

If I know that God is the Lord, not property or wealth, the possibility of peace in the world emerges, because the wealth adored by so many is the reason for war and suffering.

If I know that God is the Lord, the political, sports, showbiz, and economic *"greats"* we adore shrink back to their normal size and we do not have to bend over backwards for them to like us.

If I know that God is the Lord, I will try to discover the secrets of His creation and establish a new relationship with it instead of degrading it to a quarry of resources.

Adoration is the center of my life and everything flows from it. Adoration is not a solitary place before the Tabernacle, but in adoration I take the world before the Tabernacle. The Tabernacle is the place where God comes into the world.

Sisters of St. Francis of Perpetual Adoration

The order's name is also its agenda

The first item on the agenda is *"Francis."* When reading some of the saint's writings, one is in for a surprising discovery. The most recurrent subject in his writings is neither poverty nor fraternity nor the Church, but the Eucharist! Francis was fascinated by a God who is present in a humble morsel of bread. Hence, He has to be at the center of Franciscan spirituality and faith. Everything converges on and starts within Him.

That is why *"adoration"* is the second item on the agenda. I bow down before God who appears in the shape of a humble morsel of bread. Within this small piece of bread I discover the great God, the Creator, the Supreme and the Almighty. *"Yours are the praises, the glory, the honor, and all blessing"* (Canticle of Brother Sun). It is He whom I adore. Through adoring Him I recognize my own role: I am His creature — as are the Brother and Sister by my side and all human beings. The origin of fraternity and solidarity lies within creation.

The third item on the agenda is *"perpetual."* This is not about facing God in prayer every now and then; this is about *"perpetuation,"* forever, incessantly. Adoration becomes the central theme of my life, its leitmotif, which gives me orientation. God is in the center, *"for in Him we live and move and have our being"* (Acts 17:28).

San Damiano Prayer

Most High, Glorious God,

enlighten the darkness of my mind,

give me the right faith,

a firm hope and perfect charity,

so that I may always and in all things

act according to Your Holy Will.

Francis of Assisi

Biblical Questions and Answers

Sister: *Do you have any religious pictures that are on the wall somewhere in your home?*

Child: *Yes, we have the picture of Jesus eating his First Breakfast with some men. They had pancakes and a drink.*

Sister: *What did Jesus mean when he said, "Go out and be fishers of men"?*

Child: *That means he don't want no fishin' ladies.*

Sister: *What do you think is the reason why the Blessed Mother died?*

Answers: *She had "monia." Mary died of old age. Probably she had the flu. Maybe she had cancer. Finally a little boy raised his hand and said, "She was bit by a rattlesnake. You can see her stepping on its head." (And he pointed to the statue in the back of the room.)*

Child: *Why did the priest saw the baby when it was carried down the aisle for Baptism?*
Sister: *Where did you hear that?*
Child: *In our Reader it says: Father saw the baby with its Mother when they came into church...*

After I read a story of John the Baptist to the class ...

Child: *Sister, show us the picture of John the Baptist's head on a platter!*
Sister: *There is no picture. In those days no one had a camera or video.*

Sister: *What happened at the wedding feast of Cana?*
Child: *They ran out of wine and Jesus told Mary to do something about it. So the Blessed Mother yelled out, "Hey, you guys — get those jugs filled with water so Jesus can make more wine."*

Sister: *Who made God?*
Child: *God made the whole world and everything in it; he made Adam and Eve, too. If God made the whole world in six days, he must have been smart enough to make himself!*

"He leads - I follow"

"He leads, We follow"

Traces of Love in the Future:
The "Charitable Association of the Sisters
of St. Francis of Olpe Ltd"

The only thing of importance, when we depart,
will be the traces of love we have left behind.

(Albert Schweitzer)

"He leads, I follow"

This was the guiding principle of Mother Maria
Theresia's life and she wanted to pass her conviction
on to her Sisters. Through their tireless work the
Sisters have left traces — traces of love, traces of
prayer and traces of humanity. They were colleagues,
sympathizers, nurses, teachers, intercessors, and
human beings in one. They were caring and competent masters of their everyday lives, standing by
people with different needs and spending part of their
lives with them. All of these people, too, have left their
traces. We would like to invite you to go and look for
these traces with us.

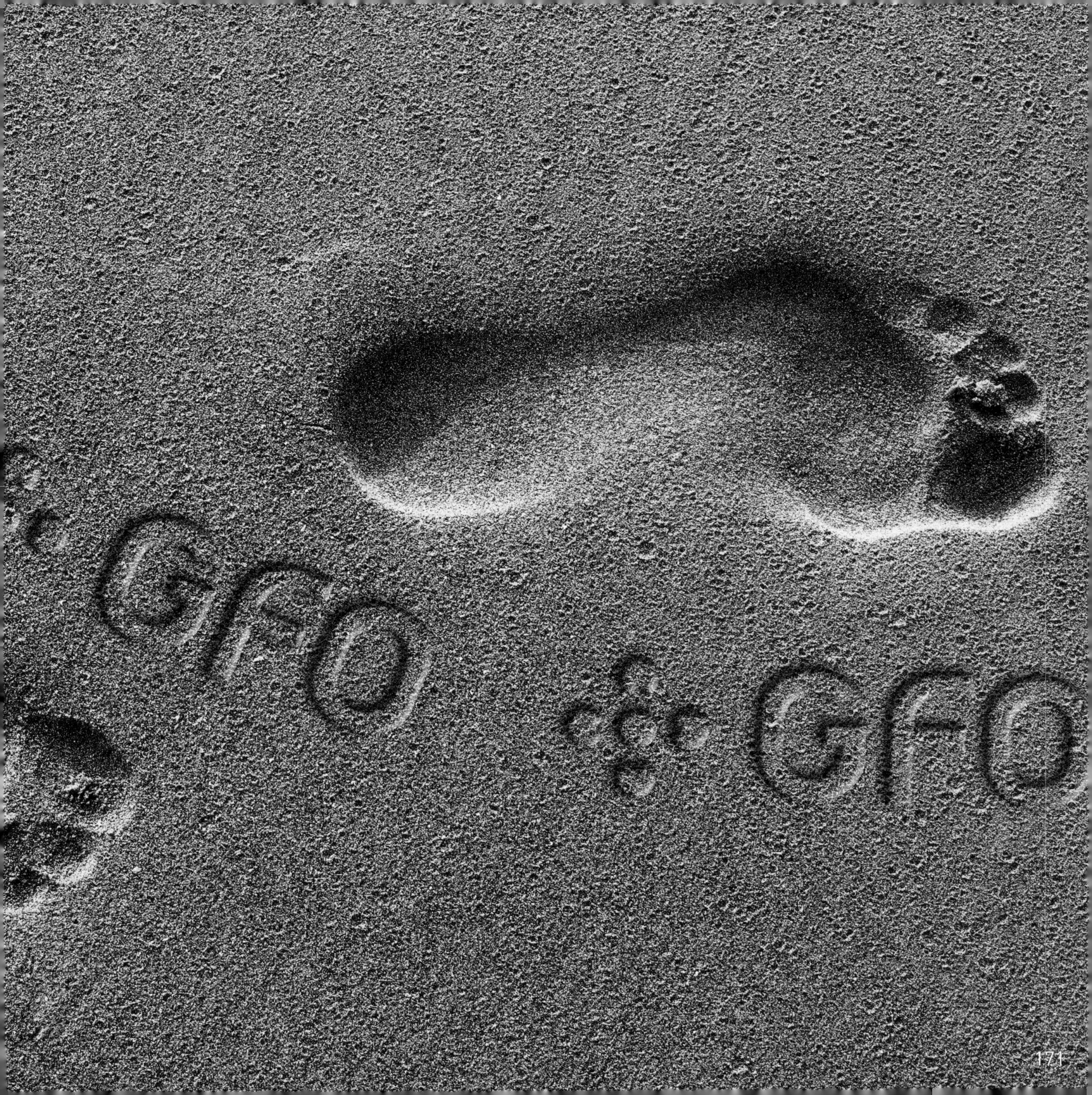

THE CHARITABLE ASSOCIATION —
MAKING DECISIONS THROUGH THE AGES

"Start by doing what is necessary; then do what is possible; and suddenly you are doing the impossible." (Francis of Assisi)

Much has changed since the order's foundation in 1863. Political, social and demographic developments have always had an impact on the lives and work of the Sisters of St. Francis of Perpetual Adoration. The Sisters have faced all changes with foresight, innovation, and a certain business sense. The new challenges in the institutions they led brought with them significant changes. These helped to ensure both the modern provision of charitable services for the public and the order's economic future. We are following traces of a successful business.

Paving the Way — the Foundation of the Limited-liability Company

With foresight, Mother Maria Theresia recognized people's needs during her 42 years as Superior and later as Superior General. She welcomed change and

spoke out for her Sisters throughout her life. She was aware of her responsibility for her life's work, and safeguarded its future remarkably early on through an important decision: in 1902, three years before her death, she founded a limited-liability company, which acted as the means of existence for her order and its institutions. From then on the Sisters' work was carried out under the name of the *"Charitable Association for Healthcare and Education of Olpe Ltd,"* as it appeared in the Commercial Register. The common capital stock of the Association was 100,000 Marks, which the five shareholders (Sr. Maria Theresia Bonzel, Sr. Raimunda Nolte, Sr. Deogratias Schäfer, Sr. Ewalda Nelz and Sr. Paula Thomas) con-

tributed equally, partly in the form of real estate. The five shareholders also acted as the company's first directors.

Securing our Path — Becoming a Registered Society

In the late 1970s the limited-liability company owned hospitals, care homes, and institutions for children and adolescents. The economic management of these institutions, in particular the state liability laws concerning hospitals, was a great financial risk for the Congregation's assets. The establishment of the registered society, *"Sisters of St. Francis*

173

of Perpetual Adoration of Olpe" in 1982 allowed for the separate administration of the company's and the Congregation's finances.

The Extension of Management

In 1983, the company owned more than 20 institutions employing around 2000 members of staff. This development posed new administrative challenges. It was barely possible to cover all personnel requirements, as regards knowledge and workload, with the Sisters. That is why, from 1983 onwards, a lay manager was brought in to co-direct the business. With this change came a slightly altered company name and purpose: "Charitable Association of the Sisters of St. Francis of Olpe Ltd."

Moving on to New Pastures — Birth of the Foundation

Mother Maria Theresia Bonzel had made the right decision in establishing the limited-liability company in the early 20th century, but 100 years later the time had come to think about change yet again. The company's economic situation was good, as the institutions had grown into a large-scale enterprise. However, the decline in the number of new Sisters joining the Congregation, and its age structure, made it impossible to meet all staffing and professional requirements with only the Sisters. Several governance models were examined before the legal status of a foundation was chosen.

The Maria Theresia Bonzel Foundation was born in 1995. The day of the arrival of the deed of foundation to the Motherhouse, July 20, 1995, became the founding day of the "Association of the Sisters of St. Francis" as well as the official founding day of the Foundation. With the transfer of the registered society's company shares to the Foundation, the latter became the shareholder and the limited-liability company remained in charge of the financial management.

The Future — Together and Without Bounds

The Sisters have carried out pioneering work for the Association's modern institutions through combining Perpetual Adoration with acts of mercy. The result is a successful company offering charitable services. The Province, though, cannot continue this success story alone — the staffing needs are too great to be covered by their comparatively small numbers of aging Sisters. Thus the Sisters keep in close contact with the Association's staff, all of whom identify with Franciscan values and principles. In the Province, the Congregation adapts to local circumstances and the demands of the time. It is a strategy in line with Mother Maria Theresia's legacy as the Association continues what was most dear to her heart: to manifest the love of God in charity, and thus to respect and support every person's dignity.

Follow us to the next pages, where we uncover some of the traces left by the Association in Mother Maria Theresia's legacy...

GFO

Yes to human dignity.

Traces of Healing

I am sitting opposite Dr. Nikolaus Ecker. I wonder how often he has sat at this table during his career, talking to patients and their families. Born in Lower Bavaria, he retired only recently after having worked in, and for most of the time co-led the anesthesia department of St. Joseph

Hospital in Troisdorf for 31 years. I do not know how you picture the work of an anesthetist, but for me he always belonged in the operating room. I seem to

be wrong. Except when he is briefing patients before or working in the operating room during surgery, the anesthetist can be found in the intensive and palliative-care units, and also in the emergency room. This has captured my interest, and I am ready to do some time travelling with Dr. Ecker.

According to his parents' wishes, Nikolaus Ecker was supposed to embark on a completely different career path. He spent five years at a convent school that

would prepare him for a role in a religious ministry later on. Yet his plans were different, and not easily accepted by his religious parents. However, his nine siblings helped him and supported his plans. The rest of his schooldays were spent at a grammar school outside the convent walls. After obtaining his medical degree in Munich, he moved to Cologne with his wife, who had been transferred there by her employer. He gained a few years' practical experience at Cologne's University Hospital before following a colleague with whom he had worked for four years to St. Joseph Hospital in Troisdorf. His work here differed greatly from what he was used to in a big university hospital.

The administrative structure was very different: the whole hospital was led by one Sister, and every ward was overseen by Sisters in leading positions. Sisters were in charge of the laboratory and operating room, too.

Dr. Ecker was impressed by the Sisters' skilled work, their experience, and their knowledge of their patients' social backgrounds. *"Back then the heads of the departments still spent a lot of time in the hospital, and yet the Sisters were already there when I arrived at work in the morning and would still be looking after the patients after I had gone home. They only interrupted their work in order to pray, eat and sleep. The time they spent with the patients was rewarded with experience and knowledge. They always knew about urgent situations and who was feeling particularly ill."* To start with, Dr. Ecker found it difficult to let go. In the beginning it was not uncommon for him to get up in the middle of the night, drive to the hospital without having been called and check that no disaster was about to happen. Nobody can cope with such a lack of sleep in the long term, and one has to learn to trust one's colleagues. Dr. Ecker and his colleague established a well-drilled team of 20. The tasks are all shared out — different colleagues are responsible for different areas such as transfusions, emergency, intensive and palliative care, etc. The team tries to stay relaxed, but the nature of the work does of course bring with it a fair amount of stress. The team members have to work well together, support each other in difficult situations and trust each other blindly. Dr. Ecker describes anesthetists as critical and ironic but with positive traits.

"I remember an experience I had during a shift I had taken on just before moving officially into my position at St. Joseph Hospital, one that made a deep impression on me. I was on duty together with a surgical nurse, a surgeon, and a student assistant when we had to make a decision: an emergency patient had come in with a rib penetrating his lungs. I examined the patient and explained to the surgeon that we really needed to operate. The surgeon trusted me and our small team successfully carried out the procedure

on the thorax. This would have been unthinkable in a university hospital of the 1970s."

Much has changed since: back then, patients were less worried before an operation. They put their trust in the medical team, who could calm them by saying *"Trust us; everything will be just fine"*. Today, it is a legal obligation to inform the patient of absolutely everything, all possible risks and complications, and the new consent forms involved do understandably produce a lot of anxiety. Moreover, it is becoming increasingly difficult to meet the expectations of patients and their families. Medicine has evolved. Today patients are being operated on who 20 years ago would have been viewed as at too great a risk of complications. To cope with the increased pressures on the staff, the hospital in Troisdorf makes sure that there is a coordinator looking after the anesthesia team on duty. When in need of advice, faced with a difficult case or unsure about a decision, the coordinator can be consulted. This way risks are kept at a minimum.

The staff at St. Joseph Hospital is especially proud of their palliative-care unit. Dr. Hosselmann, who together with Dr. Ecker had led the anesthesia department, was the one who set it up. *"If I am being honest I have to say that I had always been a little skeptical about whether we would manage to establish the unit, but my colleague never gave up. She kept her eyes on the goal, and in the end realized her vision."* Palliative medicine is important in giving terminally ill patients as high a quality of life as possible. St. Joseph Hospital

Donnerstag, 05. November

Ich Cebe Dir auch von Niklas und Paulina erzählt.
Sie leiden so sehr darunter, dass Du so krank bist.
Paulina hat den unerschütterbaren Glauben,
dass der Opa das schafft. Das weiß sie. Als ich
sie fragte, woher sie das weiß, sagte sie nur,
sie weiß es eben.

Sonntagskinder unter sich!

... Du oder
... es passiert?
... und sind über-
... oesso gut!

Freitag, 06. November
Heute bin ich dran. Ich ...
im Krankenha...
zu erkundigen. D...
Sie sehr zufrieden...
auf Ja-und Nein f...
antworten. Auch an...
Luft bekommst oder...
antwortest Du mit...
Roland und ich besuch...

Lieber Papa,
am Morgen des 23. Oktober 2005 bist ...
und entkräftet von eine verschleppt...
zusammengebrochen. Da Du ...
für eine Woche Dir auf d...
erst möchte ich Dir auf d...
zu schreiben, was in den...
Du „geschlafen" hast, ...
die ganze Situation ...
unseren Ängsten und ...
Vielleicht gibt ...
schreibe besse ...
Tage im K...

...tag, 07. Novemb...
... ich Dis...

has one of the best units in the region. The anesthesia team even does home visits now, and supports the local hospice. The work is often not easy — after all, one is accompanying people through the final stages of their lives. Yet the team is still very committed and determined to do its work well. When the palliative-care unit was opened more than ten years ago, the qualified Sisters of the intensive-care unit asked to be transferred to the new ward.

Happy moments are part of the anesthetist's work, too — e.g. when a long-term patient's condition improves after two months or when someone who had been fighting for his life for days suddenly appears at the doctor's office to thank him. The patient often has no clear memory of these difficult times, but knows about his critical condition from his family. Some patients will then use a hospital diary to trace events — it is available to all patients, and can be used by members of staff as well as the patient's loved ones during treatment. Hand-written notes record the worries, wishes, hopes and emotions of the people visiting, looking after and worrying about the patient. These moments surely leave traces in everybody's hearts.

"GROUP FRANZISKA"

TRACES OF THE FUTURE

When I ring *"Group Klara"* I am told: *"I don't want to give you Andrea's number but will ask her to ring you back if she is interested."* A few days later I find a voicemail on my cell phone; it is from Andrea. She is interested in talking to me about her life in St. Joseph's House and beyond.

Maturing traces...

The 21-year-old arrived at one of our homes when she was 14. At first she lived in *"Group Franziska,"* a supervised residential group in Attendorn-Niederhelden that is part of our Association's therapeutic-pedagogic children's home. This former farm complex is home to nine girls — just like on a real farm they look after cats, donkeys and other animals. In the beginning, Andrea had to share her room, which is never that easy, especially when it is difficult to get along with the other person and there are hardly any opportunities to spend some time alone. After a few weeks, Andrea moved into a private room and finally settled in. *"I never viewed my life 'in the home' as a punishment, because the care-takers respected and supported my wish for as much independence as possible."*

Andrea moved into *"Group Klara"* in Olpe when she was 16. Proudly she settled into her own small apartment. She prepared breakfast and dinner for herself, and after three months, she was allowed to cook alone. She learned to manage her own finances based on the pocket money and subsistence allowance she received. The experiences Andrea gained helped when she moved into her own one-bedroom apartment in Olpe — a luxury she deserves. After leaving school, during several work placements, she demonstrated her skills so well that she ended up joining a bakery's sales team as an apprentice, and passed her exams in the summer of 2010. She was promptly offered an employment contract at the bakery. Andrea's next goal is to get her driver's license, for which she is saving her money. She enjoys spending her free time wherever and with whomever she wants and is a keen swimmer.

Traces Worth Living...

Andrea really has two families: Even during her time at St. Joseph's House, she was allowed to visit her parents and older brother twice a month. Now she is free to decide when and where she wants to see them. Her Christmas, for example, was first spent with her family before visiting and spending the night in *"Group Klara,"* her *"second family:"* *"I love having friends in the group. They really helped me cope with my father's death. I have never felt ashamed about living at St. Joseph's. I have learned to speak up for myself, gained self-confidence and have been given a lot of trust. My biggest dream is having my own family."*

On the Lighter Side

Another story about reluctance of a 1st grader to come to school! After two weeks of problems happening every morning at home, I got a call from a boy's parents. The message: Tom will not get out of bed; he won't dress himself; he won't eat breakfast. We need to do all of the above and then carry him to the car; and carry him from the car to the school door! We are tired of this nonsense. We have questioned Tom about his teacher and he says he has no problem. Then they asked if I could get the "reason for his behavior or fears." So I did talk to Tom after school. He said to me, "I'm just worried about when I will be able to go home once

I get to the classroom." That was easy for me to relieve him of his worries. My reply: "Tom, every day when the school bell rings you can go home; every Friday you will go home and stay there for two days — all day Saturday and Sunday. At Christmas time, you will be home playing with all the toys Santa gives you. Then, when summer comes you will be with your mom and dad for a long time. And the best news of all is that when summer is over, you get to go to another room and be a second grader." Tom had a "million dollar smile" and perhaps a ten-pound weight off his mind. And his parents were grateful and yet surprised that Tommy had never told them about his fear.

Traces of Peace

The pretty windwheels in the garden tell many stories — stories of life, laughter, death and mourning. More than 20 windwheels keep alive the memory of the children who spent the last days of their lives in Balthasar, the children and adolescent hospice. The name of every child who passes away is written on one of the windwheel's wings; together they spin in the wind.

Balthasar is the first children's hospice of its kind in Germany, and is known beyond regional borders. Many of the children arriving here will also die here. Yet, unlike hospices for adults, the children do not only come here to die, they are often taken care of for many years. Work in a children's hospice revolves around the psychological and medical care not only of terminally ill children but also of their families. The work begins once a diagnosis has been made and continues beyond the child's death.

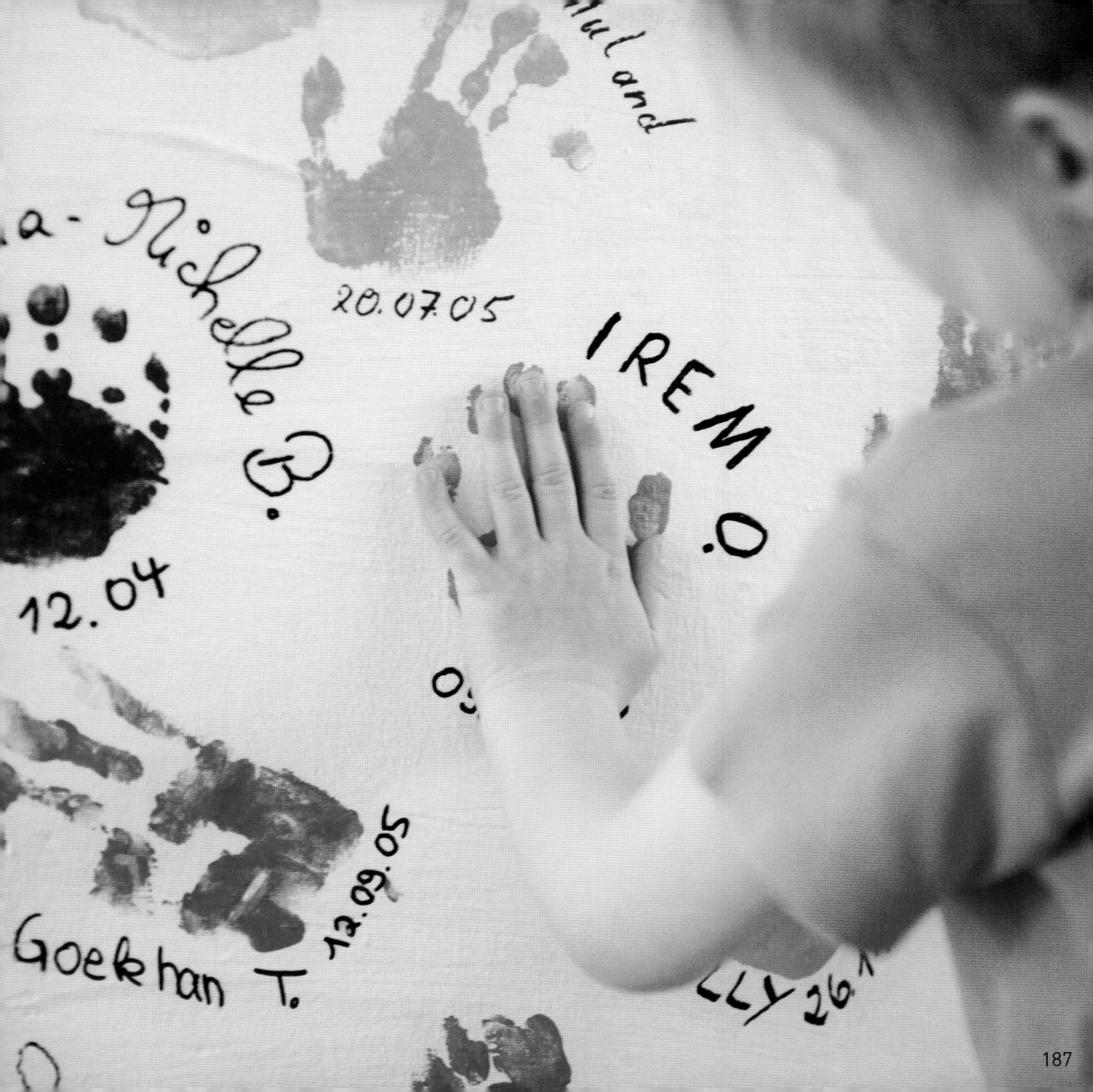
a-Michelle B.
20.07.05
IREM O.
12.04
12.09.05
Goekhan T.

Living traces

Alexander has been coming to the Children's Hospice "Balthasar" for many years. Since he was three he has been suffering from an incurable muscular disease. His muscle tissue is breaking down, and eventually his diaphragm and heart muscles will be paralyzed. Alexander has now come of age and is happy that in 2009 the hospice expanded to include adolescents. He is no longer the child who wanted to cuddle the giant teddy bears, got excited by the clowns who visited the hospice and liked to listen to stories. Just like other boys his age, he would much rather have a girlfriend, get his driving license, go to a rock concert and maybe go to a university. His healthy peers are becoming more independent of their parents and starting to go their own way. Although Alex's electric wheelchair gives him a degree of independence, he will always have to rely on the help of others, the more so the older he gets. Sometimes Alex's best friend Sebastian comes along to the hospice. Then they do what boys their age like doing: listening to loud music, watching TV for as long as and whenever they want, sitting in front of the computer, eating whatever they want to, hanging out, sleeping a lot, etc.

When Christian was 19 doctors diagnosed him with bone cancer. What was to become of his dreams? Rising up through the ranks of his football club, getting his degree, having a family?

"Dying is s**t!" Christian grapples with his fate. The hospice team deals with his grief and despair

Aline wants to know

Do you have to wake up really early?

Not that early. We begin most mornings with the Morning Prayer at 6.30am.

by responding to his questions about the meaning of death. In December 2008, Christian's condition suddenly deteriorated. Together with the hospice staff he started to plan what looked like his last Christmas — whom to invite, what kind of presents they would have and what kind of food. In the end everything was just as he had imagined. Only the snow arrived too late. At the end of Christmas Eve, Christian lay down in his bed and died the next day. It snowed on the day after Christmas.

Comforting traces

Traces and memories are important elements of mourning. Families are comforted by the thought that their children will not be forgotten. For those children and adolescents who have passed away, a *"Garden of Remembrance"* was designed in the shape of a spiral,

dying

and with stones engraved with the children's names. On every anniversary of a child's death a candle is lit, and a picture of the child, together with a personal message, are put up in one corner. There is also the guest book near the hospice's entrance, and the wall on which every child leaves his hand and footprints during his first visit to the hospice. Those who have died so young live on in these traces and in the memories of the many happy, but also difficult, moments that everyone experienced together.

The institution in Olpe remains a point of contact for the family and friends beyond the child's death, so that they continue to receive the support they need for as long as they need it.

Balthasar's window in the Room of Farewells is a place of remembrance, pain, silence, meditation, for connecting with the dead child or with God, and for being together as a family.

Almost every child knows the Three Wise Men from the nativity story. In the olden days people relied on the Men's help, and called upon them as healers of diseases of the body and mind. Even today they are considered patrons of travelers and pilgrims. In the children's hospice it is Balthasar who accompanies the children as their patron during the last phases of their lives.

Balthasar as a name means that each person follows the newborn Messiah on his journey through life. Just like the Wise Man, each soul sees its star and follows it. Balthasar embodies the longing, the journey and the destination that each person carries deep within his heart.

mourning

laughing

living

celebrating

Bill was very reluctant to say goodbye to his dad who walked him to school each morning, home for lunch, and back again when school was over for the day. They would get as far as the school door and Bill would not budge to make one more step. After a full week of this "nonsense" I decided to handle the problem once and for all! Monday morning I met Billy and Dad on the entrance steps to school. I took Billy by the arm and said, "Goodbye, Dad," but he had a different idea. Billy said, "Dad, you tell Sister to let go of my arm or I will bite her!" and I responded, "Billy, if you bite me, I will bite you and probably get a bigger hunk!" He looked at me and then at his dad and said, "Goodbye Dad, I will see you after school!" With that settled, he walked with me to the classroom. When classes were finished for the day and the kids were dismissed, I would work at my desk for 15 minutes and then go over to the church sacristy. That day, guess who was waiting for me — Billy! He held the door open and asked if he could help me up the stairway. Then he bowed to me as though I were a queen. The following Saturday, Bill and his dad came to the Convent back door with a red wagon full of groceries and goodies. His Dad said, "Sister, we were shopping today and Billy wanted you to have the same food we bought for home." They carried the items into our kitchen; Billy bowed and said, "I'll see you in Church tomorrow — and in school on Monday."

Read on about my experience of explaining the term: "we are all equal." Well, I tried to get the point across very simply to a class of 6 and 7 year olds of different races and religions. Did I succeed? You decide. Here's my story: When a doctor or nurse takes a little bit of blood from your finger, it is red no matter what color your skin shows. We are all God's children and we should be nice to each other no matter what we look like. I went on and on until I ran out of ideas. Finally, Joe raised his hand and said, "Sister, why did you say all that stuff? You could have just said — God baked those kids in the oven too long and they turned brown!" (Needless to say, the little kid thought of gingerbread boys.)

TRACES OF THE EVERYDAY

St. Konstantina, the center for the elderly in Oberpleis, is beautifully located in a vast landscaped park. Today I am meeting a member of staff who has been working at the center for a very long time. The door opens and the first thing I see is a dog's nose pushing through the gap: residents and staff love their resident dog. *"Hey, are you looking for traces, too? Have you seen Werner?"* She pricks up her ears, looks at me and wags her tail. A voice behind me says: *"Hello, I'll take you to him, he's waiting for you."* I follow my colleague, who is taking me to meet my interviewee.

I am a few minutes late, and see Werner sitting contentedly in the center's cafeteria with a cup of tea. It is not long before he starts to tell me about his life. Last November he had been working for the Charitable Association for 27 years. Back then everything was different — the many old photographs on the center's walls attest to that. In the 1970s, this was not a residence for the elderly but a hospital managed by the Sisters which also included a farm: the lawn had to be mowed, and the cows, pigs and other animals cared for on a daily basis. Even on the weekends Werner looked after the animals. He was trained in his job by the Sisters themselves. Even today many Sisters spend their retirement years in one of St. Konstantina's wings. As part of modernization plans, the hospital was turned into a home for the elderly, including a ward for more intensive-care and

assisted-living units. The barn that once stood in the yard was torn down to make way for the beautiful park and new buildings. Following this change, Werner had to take on new tasks that would also match the condition of his own health. Today he knows all the residents personally: unsurprising, seeing that he accompanies all those with walking problems to the cafeteria, is in charge of laundry and logistics, and delivers meals to the assisted-living units. Of course, changes happen regularly. Werner has so far worked under six different managers, who all introduced new

Aline wants to know

Is what you are wearing not awfully hot?

Only when it gets really hot in the summer.
We also have a dress made from a lighter material.

OLD PHOTOGRAPH OF OBERPLEIS

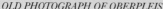

plans and ideas. This was not always easy for him. However, today he is happy; he has found his place. Colleagues accept him, residents appreciate his support, and even his free time has increased over the years. Werner reckons that his colleagues have become much nicer; now they even celebrate Carnival together. Music is his passion, and for twenty years he has been singing in a church choir. Together they have performed as far afield as Salzburg in Austria and even in Rome. When he is not singing he reads or goes on walks. Werner has three eyes when he is out and about, his own two and a third one - his digital camera, with which he captures all things beautiful. A second camera has been given to him by the choir, as he is in charge of taking pictures for their website during festivals and tours.

Werner has particularly fond memories of an extraordinary friendship: Sister Irmtrud and her Bumble-Bee. No, Bumble-Bee is no insect, she is a dog! In the mid-1990s Bumble-Bee's owner died and Sister Irmtrud "inherited" the big, black dog. From then on they were inseparable, so much so that Bumble-Bee kept Sisters Irmtrud and Gunhilde company during their long hours in the administrative office. Everyone in the center loved animals, and thus it came as no surprise that a solution was found for Bumble-Bee's own time as a senior citizen. As her walking deteriorated, she was pushed around the buildings on a tea-cart!

What a Franciscan spirit!

After a 30-minute recess following lunch, the temperature was too high to be on the play-ground, so the kids lined up to go inside and back to the classroom. I was at the end of the line to be sure there was no noise entering the building. Ahead of time, I had told the kids: do not stop to get a drink at the fountain; when we get to our desks I will call each row to go out and have a drink. So, please go directly to the room. Sure enough – what I expected to happen ... did! One girl came running up the stairs and hollered, "Hey, Babe, you ought to get down here fast. The kids are all sneaking to the fountain. They didn't listen to you."

Aline wants to know

Do you have a boyfriend?

I have very good female and male friends but no boyfriend.

THE OLD BARN

197

LUDWIG LÜTTIKE

TRACES OF LIFE

Yesterday was the day after Christmas. My plan was to visit Ludwig Lütticke at St. Gerhardus in Drolshagen last week, but the heavy snow made it impossible to reach the town by car. What I did not know then: the snow and Christmas have a special significance for Mr. Lütticke. A colleague takes me to meet him and he welcomes me with a big smile from his soft, bright eyes. His daughter-in-law is visiting him, too. I introduce myself, and a few minutes later find myself sitting opposite Mr. Lütticke. I relax and

start to feel very much at ease in the 84-year-old's presence. He starts to tell me about the traces that people and events have left in his heart and mind throughout his long life.

Red Traces

"My daughter invited me to spend Christmas Eve with her and her family. It was wonderful; we had rabbit for dinner," he tells me. A lovely Christmas Eve

ASSISTED-LIVING UNITS IN DROLSHAGEN

surrounded by family; life has not always been that kind to him.

His thoughts drift to the terrifying Christmas Eve of 1944. The then 18-year-old is stationed in Normandy, where he has been deployed for the third time, just before Christmas. It is snowing, the temperature is low, and he and his fellow soldier Hermann are nervously waiting in the foxhole right at the front. Hermann will not celebrate Christmas. He gets hit in the head by a bullet and dies right next to Ludwig. There is no way out for Ludwig this time, neither out of the foxhole nor away from his dear friend's dead body. Crying, he waits to be called back, although this means leaving his comrade behind. Five days later, on Christmas Eve, Ludwig is with other soldiers and feels terribly homesick. After a cigarette, some mulled wine and chocolate, the five soldiers take up patrol duty. Everything suddenly happens very quickly: a blinding light, not the Star of Bethlehem but certain death for three soldiers. Ludwig and another comrade manage to escape the hail of bullets and look for shelter on the ground. Another ray of light! This time it is a grenade, and although the two soldiers instinctively jump out of the light they get hit by splinters. The snow turns red; screams and cries for help are heard in the night. Suddenly the shooting stops and, unbelievably, *"Silent Night"* is sung on the other side. Finally Ludwig is rescued by his comrades. He slowly recovers.

Years of Privations...

Although his toes were badly frostbitten, it was decided that Ludwig had to return to the front. This decision resulted not only in more nightmares but also in years of privations. At first he was captured by the Soviets. The soldiers cooped him in a cage; he was expecting the worst. But Ludwig managed the impossible; he escaped. I am surprised to hear him say *"Russians are very gentle people; that is how I experienced them, unless you anger them."* Eventually he was captured by the French, and he and the other prisoners had to build the camp's fencing and watchtowers with their own hands.

WEDDING PHOTO OF REGINA AND LUDWIG LUTTIKE

The camp was to be Ludwig's *"home"* for more than three years. Life there was hard, he says, but not heartless. He has stayed friends with two of his former *"guards"* to this day, and used to visit them in France. *"Many of the Frenchmen had a good heart. Although we had to work, we were allowed to learn English and French for one hour a day. Those who made an effort received an extra plate of watery soup."* Still, at 1.88 meters tall, he only weighed 44 kilograms when he finally returned home in 1947. He remembers his younger sister saying: *"Mommy, is the gentleman going to stay with us?" "Yes,"* his mother replied, *"he is your big brother."* His sister simply could not remember her brother.

In Love...

After the war, Ludwig occasionally went to the theater in Wegeringhausen. The beautiful tall actress caught his eye immediately and he said to his sister: *"One day this girl will be my wife."* His sister burst out laughing and replied: *"You're crazy!"* No, Ludwig was not crazy, he simply had a big heart and Regina, the actress, noticed that very quickly. They married in 1952, raised three children and spoiled seven grandchildren. *"We were married for 56 years and I never regretted it for* one second," the trained carpenter tells me. "*I built our house myself with the help of my wife; first, she would feed our first child and then return to mixing the mortar. We were a great team.*"

Traces Worth Living...

A week after their golden wedding anniversary, Regina suffered a stroke and remained in need of care for the following five years. She spent this time at St. Gerhardus. "*Her care could not have been better. I knew my wife was in the best hands imaginable and I could visit her whenever I wanted. During the last*

On the Lighter Side

Every morning, the principal would have each teacher send a report to her office concerning certain information: count of absentees, milk orders, and hot lunches. We also had to submit a simple survey of family information. This survey was necessary just once a year; and it was not easy for first graders to understand. The principal always wondered why it took so long for the report to be sent to her secretary. One day I said to her, "Come and see and hear what goes on in the first grade room during the 'question and answer' period before classes begin."

- **Question:** "Sue, are you the oldest child in the family attending this school?"
- **Answer:** "Yes, but my dad is the oldest one in the family."
- **Question:** "Sue, do you have a sister or brother in this school?"
- **Answer:** "My brother did come but he ain't six here anymore. My sister ain't six old enough yet."
- **Question:** "Sue, how many children are in your family?"
- **Answer:** "There are three but mommy says there's one on the way; and my dog is treated like one of us. He is older than me."

(The Sister Principal had come to my room for a short time; before the analysis was completed she walked out and declared she wouldn't be back for another session like that.)

years I rented an assisted-living flat on the premises and could see her every day." Ludwig moved to the care home a few months ago and feels well looked after. He has been suffering from diabetes for sixty years, and has also had several bypasses and stent implants. Ludwig has to continue his life here without the love of his life, but he who sows love will reap it. During our interview two young men appear in the doorway and lovingly say hello to their grandfather. I imagine them to be the two "airmen" who once took to the skies with their granddad and showed him the center from above. Ludwig, who suffered a war and privations as a young man, is very happy that his grandchildren can enjoy their youth. His children and their families visit him often. He is never bored, as he takes part in many of the activities offered at St. Gerhardus, enjoys the delicious and varied meals and receives Holy Communion. Due to having collapsed several times, he can only visit the chapel occasionally, and Communion is brought to him. In the old days, when he was healthy, he never missed a Mass. "I often see the Sisters in the cafeteria. I am a cheerful person, and they call me 'Uncle Ludwig'."

"I like the staff and the Sisters at St. Gerhardus. I love living here." I am not surprised that everyone likes such a warm-hearted and open-minded person! Such a person will leave traces, I am sure. He has already left them in my heart.

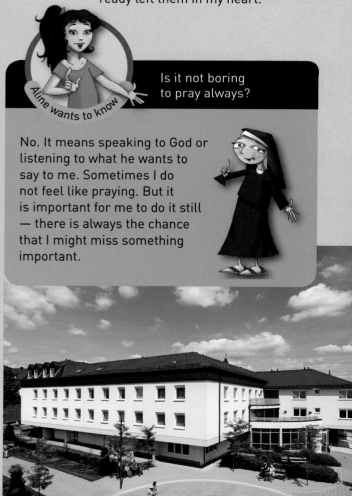

Aline wants to know

Is it not boring to pray always?

No. It means speaking to God or listening to what he wants to say to me. Sometimes I do not feel like praying. But it is important for me to do it still — there is always the chance that I might miss something important.

ST. GERHARDUS IN DROLSHAGEN

"He leads - I follow"

CHAPTER **XII**   AN INTERVIEW WITH THE ORDER'S
OLDEST SISTER

Interview with Sr. Richardis Durant, 29th of October 2010,
3 days after her 105th birthday.

SCG: (SISTER CLARICE GENTRUP, INTERVIEWER)

SR. R: (SISTER RICHARDIS)

SCG (Sister Clarice Gentrup, interviewer):

What motivated you to enter Religious Life and specifically our congregation?

Sr. R: (Sister Richardis):

I heard about Franciscans during a retreat is San Bernadino, California.

I always had a special love for the Sisters of St. Francis because they cared for my family in New Mexico. I met them during High School in Gallup, New Mexico.

SCG:

Of what importance has the Spirituality of St. Francis and Mother Theresia been for you?

Sr. R:

St. Francis's conversion and deep love of God not only inspired me but attracted me. The whole of the life of Francis has importance for me. I always had the feeling I was called to pray for the conversion of sinners. I was born the year Mother Theresia died. I always felt that I was her child. She died in February, and I was born in October.

MOUNT SAINT FRANCIS 1954

On the Lighter Side

After having lunch at home, Cory came back to school and met me on the playground. He had a definite concern on his mind. Cory said, "Sister, I know how to work problems like 2+3 and 3+5; but on the sidewalk I saw a different kind of problem that I could not figure out. In a heart-shaped picture it says Sue + Tom. I simply answered his concern: "Don't worry, Cory, because you will never see that in our math workbook."

SCG:
What were highlights for you in the course of your years in community?

Sr. R:
I was Academic Dean at the University of Albuquerque for 15 years. When it was time to be transferred, I wanted to spend more time with Scripture and God, so I asked if I could work in Religious Education. I was 63 years of age when I was given a ministry where I had 1800 public school students and 100 volunteer teachers. I was there for 15 years, until I was 78 years old. It was the best time of my life.

SCG:
What encouraged you to remain in our community?

Sr. R:
I have never been tempted to leave the convent.

SCG:
What made you happy?

Sr. R:
I always was happy. When I entered the convent and stood by the window in my convent bedroom that night, I felt that if all girls in the world knew the happiness I felt at that time, there would not be enough convents to hold them all.

SCG:
What weighed heavily on your mind?

Sr. R:
I don't think anything did. I was always at peace. When I was in my thirties, I needed a colostomy and I've lived with it for 70 years. It always was a cross. I feel God carried that cross with me. I feel in the end it will be my greatest glory. I have always been healthy, seldom suffering from illness until now. I consider myself to have been blessed with extraordinarily good health.

SCG:
How do you experience our community today?

Sr. R:
I am sad to see our diminishment in numbers. Maybe God has a different plan for our Congregation. (far away look in her eyes - maybe sad look)

SCG:
What do you regard as your task?

Sr. R:
I believe I am called to pray for the conversion of sinners. I pray the Divine Mercy Chaplet every night, so that someone who is dying will have the grace to make peace with God.

SCG:
How do you envision the future of our community?

Sr. R:
That is a repeat. Maybe God has a different direction for us now that lay people are doing so much of what the Sisters did in the past. I have deep faith in God and trust that God is leading us.

Aline wants to know

Is this your car?

No. The car belongs to the community and I am using it because I need it for work.

SCG:

What do you think you can convey to people today through your vocation? Initially she said she wasn't around people any longer, so I asked about the people who come to see her, and she said—

Sr. R:

I try to accept each one who comes into my room to help me, as they are, so they will feel good about themselves. I do not let them know that I think they aren't doing some things correctly.

SGC:

Is there a legacy, a sentence, an act of our foundress which is especially important to you?

Sr. R:

Our Congregation's enduring devotion to St. Joseph.

SCG:

Do you see a thread (a theme) which has endured throughout the Congregation since the foundation until today?

Sr. R:

I can't say that I do. End.

Note:

Sr. Richardis was born on October 26, 1905.
The interview took place on October 29, 2010.
She died on October 20, 2011.

212

On the Lighter Side

Leo was a rather shy little boy. He preferred to walk around with the playground supervisor rather than join in fun games with his classmates. He feared, at times, that others would make fun of him. When he became second grader, after a few months into the school year, his mom asked him, "How are you doing on the playground with the other kids, Leo?" He said, "Mom, I remember in the first grade, Sister Robertann told us that in the Bible it says: We should forgive others 70 times 7. And I'm almost up to that number!"

On the Lighter Side

As a substitute in Grade Two, after completing a lesson in Religion, a little boy came to me and said, "Sister, I didn't know that you knew so much about God!" I responded, "Oh, thank you Alex. I could teach you all night long about God." He looked at me and replied, "No, let's wait until morning comes."

213

On the Lighter Side

The Finale of Teaching Days

After explaining the Good Shepherd story from the first grade religion book (in simple terms), I stressed that the Good Shepherd was not so much concerned about the lamb on His shoulder; he is looking for ninety-nine sheep that were not with the whole flock. Then I compared that with the idea that Jesus is looking for the people that are not in church for Sunday Mass! He knows if your family had other plans for the day.

A concerned little girl came to my desk and asked: "Does the Good Shepherd come on Saturday evening to see who is in Church?" I assured her that the Good Shepherd and I see your parents, you, and your four sisters in the front pew every Saturday evening for Mass. She was so relieved!

The first graders loved to pantomime bible stories. Throughout the school year, we would manage to set aside a time for "show and tell" what we know! This was a volunteer activity for the children who chose to participate; the other children would "guess" what bible story the "brave" classmates were imitating. Of the many "pantomimes," the following one was the most popular and hilarious!

Two classroom buddies volunteered to pantomime the bible story concerning "Gambling in the Temple." They sat at the table in front of the room. Nate and Mike were enjoying the act of dealing cards to each other and winning or losing chips! The boys had forgotten to choose a classmate to be Jesus, so I took over to complete the scene. I did what Jesus had done: tipped over the chairs and table gently, as well as the cards and chips. Nate and Mike were stunned and frightened. One of the boys said, "Sister, we did what the bible says; what did we do wrong?" I assured them they did a great job. Then I reminded them that Jesus was in the Temple, also. And Jesus did not approve of what was going on in the House of Prayer! Their classmates clapped and cheered for such a great act.

Once a parent informed me that her son and three of his friends often pretended that they were celebrating a funeral Mass. One boy chose to be the priest, two boys volunteered to be servers, and the other child was the "dead" person. This went on for a good period of time in the home of one of the boys. Then there was a sudden "stop" for all four children. Finally, the subject came up again. Mom said, "Luke, why aren't your friends having 'funerals' anymore?" He answered, "I quit because I was tired of always pretending that I'm dead."

Years ago I was walking to town. I passed a parking lot and saw three young children in a car. The windows were open and they were calling me. So I walked over to them and said, "I could not understand what you were saying." All of them said, "Hi, God!" I said, "Hi", and walked away, (forgetting to tell them I wasn't God).

Remember the days of Sister Bertrille? A little kindergartener asked me if I came down from heaven dressed like a nun. Then he added, "I saw her flying in the movie, and I wondered if you can fly, too?"

" He leads - I follow "

CHAPTER **XIII** AN INTERVIEW WITH THE ORDER'S YOUNGEST SISTERS

All novices filled in a questionnaire, from which the following answers were chosen.

NOVICES AND POSTULANTS

What motivated you to join our congregation?

At first I was attracted by the habit. Upon meeting a few Sisters I liked their cheerfulness, contentedness and simple life.

What attracts you to St. Francis's and Mother Maria Theresia's spirituality?

I am attracted by St. Francis's love for Lady Poverty. He gave up his wealth to follow Christ. I also admire Mother Maria Theresia's courage when faced with problems and challenges, her attitude to prayer and her motherliness.

What problems have you experienced during your life in the community?

Adjusting to different personalities, and being apart from my family.

What has encouraged you to stay in our community?

The thought that I can best serve God in this way of living, and the prospect of growing in my spirituality; that I have time for prayer, Mass and contemplation.

What makes you happy?

I am happiest when I am with my Sisters, when we pray together and I receive Jesus every day. I am happy about my vocation to be here.

What do you consider to be important about your vocation in our community?

Perpetual adoration is very important to me and my vocation within the community.

On the Lighter Side

Little Mark came to my desk with a message: "Sister, my mom told me to let you know that I will be absent from school for a couple of days. She is taking me to the Mayo Clinic." When I asked how he was feeling, he responded, "I'm okay but mom wants to ask the doctor how many 'marbles' I have!" (Actually, I knew Mark's mom was concerned about his mental ability). On Monday morning Mark returned to school. He walked into the classroom and came directly to my desk. With a big smile he said, "Hey, Sister, guess what happened...the doctor found almost eight marbles!"

How do you experience our community today?

Although life in the community is still relatively new to me, I am experiencing mutual understanding, contentedness and joy among the Sisters despite the hard work they put into their apostolate. I see them taking time for conversations with each other, and admire the way the Sisters live and look after us younger ones.

What do you consider your task or role in community life?

I pray for the Sisters, and try to be good and do what is expected of me as their Sister.

How do you see our community's future?

If every Sister continues what the older Sisters have begun, then she will spread Mother Maria Theresia's charisma further. By practicing their apostolate for the good of the community, the Sisters live the life that is expected of them. If every Sister strives to live according to the Gospel, then we will be successful and attract others so that they may join our community, which will continue to serve others.

A POSTULANT JOINS THE NOVITIATE, INVESTITURE INTO THE HABIT

Aline wants to know

Where do you go on a holiday?

I visit my relatives for a few days, or go somewhere nice like another convent in Germany.

How can you attract others through your vocation?

Through the life I live as a Sister.

Which legacy, deed or quote of our foundress is most important to you?

What I find most impressive about our Mother Foundress is the fact that she is a shepherdess of souls who guides young women towards God in order to serve, love and admire Him, and to help the poor, unfortunate children.

Aline wants to know

My mom says you are not allowed to smoke or drink beer. Is that true?

Yes that is true. We are not allowed to smoke; but we drink beer with dinner on special occasions.

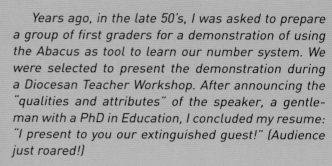

On the Lighter Side

The last laugh is on the teacher

Years ago, in the late 50's, I was asked to prepare a group of first graders for a demonstration of using the Abacus as tool to learn our number system. We were selected to present the demonstration during a Diocesan Teacher Workshop. After announcing the "qualities and attributes" of the speaker, a gentleman with a PhD in Education, I concluded my resume: "I present to you our extinguished guest!" (Audience just roared!)

In those same early 50's, as a young Sister and teacher, I walked to the Kresges store in town. Before entering the building, I noticed an interesting display in the storefront window: a Borden cow churning out two flavors of Kraft Caramels! Evidently, I was smiling and showing so much joy...the manager met me outside and said, "Sister, I see you are enthused about our display! Here, enjoy these," and he handed me a whole carton of caramels. I forgot all about shopping.

Another day I decided to shop at Woolworth's for some great sales. There seemed to be a lack of clerks to help me find what I wanted and its cost. After wandering around the store, I noticed a well-dressed lady, so I walked toward her and asked for a little help. No response. So I went to another well-dressed lady. No response. Finally, it dawned on me: those silent women were mannequins. Dummy! ☺

On a cold, icy day I went shopping with a Sister Superior. She decided to shop at a different store, and asked me to meet her at Penney's across the street. About ten minutes later I left the store, went to the street corner, got to the curb of the intersection, and then slipped on the ice; and naturally, I fell down and hit my head! I managed to get up and support myself on the pillar of the bank building. Thank the Lord there was no traffic at the intersection when I fell. But, a gentleman saw me; he parked his car and came to the building to see if I needed help. I replied, "No, Sir, I'm waiting for a Sister to come from Penney's. She will see me and take me home." So the kind man asked me a few questions: "Are you a Roman Catholic?" "Yes, Sir." "Do you believe in God?" "Yes, Sir, I do." "Do you believe in Jesus?" "Yes, I do." Do you believe He is your Lord and Savior?" "Yes, Sir, I do." "Do you believe you will go to heaven when you die?" I responded, "Sir, if I fall many more times this year I will get there sooner than I think!" With that he got back in his car and drove off.

In the early 60's I was a graduate student at the University of Dayton (in Ohio). One of the courses I had in Educational Psychology entailed giving a speech. We also had to name the source from which we obtained the material; and if we used direct quotes, that had to be acknowledged. Loud and clear I announced: This quote is taken directly from Pluto, and my reference was the Mine Magazine. Thereafter, on campus I was known as Sister Pluto, and every teacher in the class knew the Mine Magazine was for primary grades!

A favorite episode that our Provincial loves to hear over and over again concerns myself. In the summertime I would be at the Motherhouse in July. Each summer the South Bend Clinic needed volunteer blood donors; so in my younger days, I would donate blood each summer. I will never forget my "first" time as a donor. I had to answer a questionnaire verbally. The clinician asked:

Are you involved in a risky job? (Yes, I teach school during the year and wash windows in a tall building in the summertime.)

Have you ever been rejected? (A few times, but I got over it.)

At that point the lady said to me; "Sister, that question refers to your blood!" Turning red-faced instantly I said, "My blood has always been accepted." After a few summers as a donor, the Provincial said, "Why do you like to donate blood?" My response: "Because they give me cookies and orange juice before they send me home!" All the listeners laughed, knowing I could (and do) have the same treat here.

Often we hear the famous and familiar words; "out of the mouths of babes..." I have chosen to conclude my teaching experiences with three occasions applicable to the above quote.

1) During an art lesson I always tried to encourage the children to enjoy drawing simple pictures. We would take one step at a time to draw a house, a sailboat, a scenery of trees, etc. After a period of time the class became at ease. One day in the midst of drawing a picture, Dan said, "Sister, we can draw almost as good as you do!"

2) In a math class I wrote a problem on the blackboard: 2+3=5. Joey raised his hand and said, "Hey, Sister, that answer is wrong." I invited him to come to the board and teach me how to figure out answers the way I taught the class. He drew 000+00 and began to count the circles. "I see 3 circles and 2 more." When he came up with 5 (with a surprising look on his face), he said, "Teacher, you're right."

3) For grammar lessons, I occasionally put five sentences on the board with an error in each one. Anyone could respond to any sentence. After two responses were given correctly, Mary says, "Sentence number 3 is crooked."

THE LAST LAUGH

The amazing career of teaching first graders
for 50 years (without a single day
of absenteeism due to illness)
was truly rewarding!
I began thinking about retiring
when a child said:
"I know you taught my mother;
did you teach my grandpa, too?"

Publisher:

Éditions du Signe

1 rue Alfred Kastler - Eckbolsheim

B.P. 94 – 67038 Strasbourg, Cedex 2, France

Tel: ++33 (0) 3 88 78 91 91

Fax: ++33 (0) 3 88 78 91 99

www.editionsdusigne.fr

Email: info@editionsdusigne.fr

Edited by: Generalate
  Sister Magdalena Krol OSF

Authors: Sister Magdalena Krol OSF -
  Hildegard Nies - Nicole Fries - Sr. Laurentiana Antpöhler (+2006) -
  Sr. Rose Agnes Pfautsch - Sr. M. Stephanie McReynolds - Sr. Emilie Igano -
  Sr. Francisca Rodrigues do Vale and Sr. Marie José Silva dos Santos -
  P. Heribert Arens OFM - Sr. Clarice Gentrup - Sr. Judith Lorica

Pictures: • Photos from Sisters of St. Francis of Perpetual Adoration, Olpe
  • p.14 Josef Schmitd, Westfahlenpost Olpe
  • Cornelius Gotthardt
  • Birgitte Petershagen
  • Stephanie Alker
  • René Traut
  • Tim Friesenhagen
  • Christian Schmitz
  • Fotolia.com : © openlens; © CLIPAREA.com; p. 2: © danimages; p. 9: © Maksym
    Dykha; p. 12: © Anatoliy Terebenin; p. 30: © Rodoudou; p. 40: © alma_sacra;
    p. 43: © Barmaliejus; p. 54: © Undine Aust; p. 66: © TheGame; p. 78: © EF-EL;
    p. 80: © Regor Imperator; p. 100: © Lynne Nicholson; p. 152: © Paul Lemke;
    p. 158: © Bo Valentino; p. 162: © emmi; p. 165: © Alexey Kardakov; p. 166:
    © Subbotina Anna; p. 168: © Leonid Tit; p. 170: © iggyphoto; p. 172: © Alexey
    Klementiev; p. 173: © Michael Nivelet; p. 175, 176: © Alx; p. 177: © John Keith;
    p. 178: © Birute Vijeikiene; p. 181: © A. Pospiech; p. 183: © Peter LECKO; p. 193:
    © pressmaster; p. 194: © Mikael Damkier; p. 204: © Toutenphoton; p. 206:
    © Luminis; p. 214: © Prod. Numérik; p. 215: © galam; p. 216: © Grischa Georgiew;
    p. 226: © Marzanna Syncerz; p. 228: © Laurence Gough; p. 230: © Luana Rigolli

Illustrations: François Ruyer, Eric Herr

Layout: Anthony Kinné – Éditions du Signe